GV
884
.J67
A34
1999

NOV ´´ ´´ 2001

BEVERL

SO-AHV-557

RO176232032

Michael Jordan speaks : lessons from the

MICHAEL JORDAN
SPEAKS

Lessons

from the

World's Greatest

Champion

~ ❋ ~

CHICAGO PUBLIC LIBRARY
BEVERLY BRANCH
1962 W. 95TH STREET
CHICAGO, IL 60643

MICHAEL JORDAN SPEAKS

Lessons

from the

World's Greatest

Champion

JANET LOWE

CHICAGO PUBLIC LIBRARY
BEVERLY BRANCH
1962 W. 95TH STREET
CHICAGO, IL 60643

John Wiley & Sons, Inc.

New York • Chichester • Weinheim • Brisbane • Singapore • Toronto

This book is printed on acid-free paper. ⊚

Copyright ©1999 by Janet Lowe. All rights reserved.

Published by John Wiley & Sons, Inc.
Published simultaneously in Canada.

No part of this publication may be reproduced, stored in a retrieval
system or transmitted in any form or by any means, electronic,
mechanical, photocopying, recording, scanning or otherwise, except
as permitted under Sections 107 or 108 of the 1976 United States
Copyright Act, without either the prior written permission of the
Publisher, or authorization through payment of the appropriate
per-copy fee to the Copyright Clearance Center, 222 Rosewood Drive,
Danvers, MA 01923, (978) 750-8400, fax (978) 750-4744. Requests
to the Publisher for permission should be addressed to the Permissions
Department, John Wiley & Sons, Inc., 605 Third Avenue, New York,
NY 10158-0012, (212) 850-6011, fax (212) 850-6008, E-Mail:
PERMREQ@WILEY.COM.

This publication is designed to provide accurate and authoritative
information in regard to the subject matter covered. It is sold
with the understanding that the publisher is not engaged in rendering
professional services. If professional advice or other expert assistance
is required, the services of a competent professional person should
be sought.

This book has not been prepared, approved, licensed, or endorsed
by Michael Jordan.

Library of Congress Cataloging-in-Publication Data:
Lowe, Janet
    Michael Jordan speaks: lessons from the world's greatest champion /
by Janet Lowe.
       p.   cm.
    Includes bibliographical references.
    ISBN 0-471-34564-4 (cloth : alk. paper)

Book design and composition by Anne Scatto / PIXEL PRESS

Printed in the United States of America

10   9   8   7   6   5   4   3   2   1

~ ✳ ~

This book is dedicated to those
truly good sports in our lives,
Sarah, Nicole, and Charlie
Brandon, Tarah, and Austin

~ ✳ ~

CHICAGO PUBLIC LIBRARY
BEVERLY BRANCH
2121 W. 95TH ST   60643

CONTENTS

PREFACE

Sports fans love statistics, and for basketball superstar Michael Jordan, the statistics might seem to tell it all. He has won 6 National Basketball Association Championship rings, 5 Most Valuable Player trophies, won the scoring title 10 times, played on All-Star teams, and participated in two Olympic events, from which he took home 2 gold medals.

But anyone who has seen the 6-foot 6-inch athlete on the court knows there is more to the legendary MJ than numbers. A fan, William J. Demorascki of Glendale, Arizona, tried to explain, in responding to an article in *Time* magazine. "'His Airness' is a tiger on the court: all flowing power, amazing grace, and indomitable will. Off the court, he is warm, and comports himself with dignity and style, keeping a bit of mystery about himself," said Demorascki. "Because he doesn't engage in the excesses and on- and off-court buffoonery of [former] teammate Dennis Rodman, you say he is bland. Jordan is one of the greatest personalities of this or any other century. Millions of fans watch him mesmerized for one reason: the force of his presence holds us."[1]

Jordan is like a jackhammer when he runs down the gymnasium floor, playing hard, and incessantly intimidating his opponents with trash talk. But he knows how far to go and where to draw the line. He can tease, he can cut up and be funny—in short, he charms audiences who watch games from the stands or on television. Those who visit Michael Jordan's, the Restaurant, a virtual shrine decorated with hundreds of larger-than-life photographs of Jordan, realize that physically, the man is a work of art.

~

No wonder Jordan has come to represent a cultural ideal, especially to young people. His stature enables him to be a sports marketing machine, a valuable commodity particularly to companies that hire him to hawk their products.

According to *Advertising Age*, Jordan was a pioneer in sports marketing. He "virtually singlehandedly created the modern sports marketing industry and transformed the role of celebrity endorsers."[2]

Jordan sometimes has sounded surprised by his own ability to move goods and services off the shelf. When he was named the *Sporting News'* Most Powerful Person in Sports for 1997, Jordan said he felt his power mainly when he stepped out on the basketball court.

"I never view myself as powerful enough to make decisions or influence business. It's just that, for whatever reason, the public and corporate America have accepted my personality."[3]

~

The public's desire to know every detail about the former guard for the Chicago Bulls created a flourishing industry for the media. The basketball star's name has seemed ubiquitous, appearing in an average of 100 newspaper articles a day during the time he was playing basketball. When Jordan announced his final retirement from basketball on January 13, 1999, the *Chicago Tribune* reported that it had mentioned its basketball hero 13,987 times since 1986. And more than 70 books have been published about—or by—Jordan.

Writing about Jordan in *GQ*, Charles N. Pierce said, "The great conundrum is that he is so radical in his play and so conventional in his daily life. He is a family man, a chronic golfer, a pure capitalist and now even a cartoon character, in the movie *Space Jam*."[4]

Despite the billions of words written about Jordan, *Wall Street Journal* writer Allen Barra noted how hard it is to get a vector reading on MJ's personality. "Michael Jordan is the most written-about athlete of the '90s and yet one of the least known. Over the past few years, in fact, he seems to have undergone a unique reverse metamorphosis of stardom: The more we hear about him, the less we feel we know him. Mr.

Jordan may indeed be the herald of a new kind of celebrity, one that grows more out of focus the longer the camera is on him."[5]

The Reverend Jesse Jackson, a Bulls fan, says that Jordan has handled fame and success well, something that sports figures have a notoriously difficult time managing. "Michael has used his power not to elevate himself, but to extend himself—that's unusual," Jackson said.[6]

Despite the accolades, Jordan has shown human fallibility as well. He is competitive to the extreme, which works for him on the court, but can cause him to be hard on his teammates if they don't perform. And Jordan's penchant for gambling on golf and card games has led to investigations by the National Basketball Association, and although it was clear that Jordan at times lost large sums of money, the NBA didn't find he'd acted unethically. Some critics claimed while Jordan was a role model on the court and a generous philanthropist, he did not do enough for the black community. Football Hall of Famer Jim Brown once called Jordan a "white black man who forgets about his brothers."[7]

But none of the criticism diminished public admiration for Jordan. It was with sorrow and dismay that sports fans received the news in 1999 that Jordan would be retiring.

"It would be easy to say that Jordan has been a one-man industry," wrote the *Washington Post*'s Joel Achenbach, "but he's really been more like a utility, a piece of the national infrastructure, important to daily life as the storm sewer grid. This is a reminder that things that pe granted—Ma Bell, the Soviet Union, Micha on Sunday afternoons—can disappear suddenly."[8]

It is unlikely, however, that Michael Jordan will disappear from public view. He's only taking a breather. The former sports star is too valuable a resource— to himself, to marketers, and to his admirers—to remain unseen. Jordan, some say, needs to be out where he can be visible, and the life of an actor may be perfect for him now. His first movie role was in *Space Jam*, a combination cartoon/live action film for children, and it was a success. Jordan shows progressively better acting skills in his television commercials. In all likelihood, he soon will become a familiar figure to moviegoers, perhaps appearing in walk-on parts, cameos, and starring in films written especially for him. He may not disappear from basketball altogether; only weeks after retiring he began talking about buying a team.

～

In *Michael Jordan Speaks*, the superstar's remarkable life story is told primarily in his own words, with quotations culled from thousands of sources. Remember please that Jordan did not make these comments in the order that they are presented here. Rather, the quotes have been arranged so as to create a story and paint a picture of a complex and completely original

...ican. For details on where and when Jordan said ...mething, refer to the notes at the back of the book.

This book is the sixth in the *Speaks* series. Before Michael Jordan, I wrote books in the same format about Warren Buffett, the world's most successful investor; Jack Welch, chairman of General Electric and the world's most successful manager; Bill Gates, founder of Microsoft and the world's most effective entrepreneur; talk-show host Oprah Winfrey, one of the most influential voices in the world; and Billy Graham, the world's most beloved evangelist.

Like the others, Jordan came from an ordinary American background. He grew up in a small city, attended a state college, and was the first in his family to gain prominence. Like the others, Jordan found his calling early in life, then patiently and persistently followed his dream to reach the pinnacle. He had natural talent, but he worked hard, polishing his skills as if they were precious stones. When problems dogged him, he held steady.

Finally, like the others in the *Speaks* series, Jordan's story assures us that the American dream can still be achieved. One of the main purposes of this book is to show how Jordan rose to his level of achievement and excellence, and how he copes with the pressures of performance, fame, and wealth.

~

A number of people made important contributions to this book. Lynne Carrier deserves special recognition for her research work and collaboration in putting *Michael Jordan Speaks* together. She was very thorough; in fact, she got so involved in the subject that she joined an adult women's basketball program and still is playing.

Special thanks to Myles Thompson, Jennifer Pincott, Heather Florence, and Robin Goldstein at John Wiley & Sons Inc. Without their attention to detail and dedication to quality, we all would be lost. My literary agent, Alice Fried Martell, has been with me every step of the way in all my book projects, including this one. Jolene Crowley of Crowley Communications has listened patiently and made many fine suggestions for the manuscript. My husband and helpmate Austin Lynas made countless trips to the library and to the Internet, gathering more information. He read the manuscript, fielded telephone calls, and worked on the tax returns while I was otherwise occupied. Thanks to all these people for being on my team.

~

From working on this book we've learned that Michael Jordan is both an ordinary human being and a genuine hero, and there is much to learn from his life. May you enjoy reading this book as much as we have enjoyed preparing it.

Janet Lowe
Del Mar, California
MARCH 1999

A LITTLE
HARDSHIP EARLY

To basketball superstar Michael Jordan, his life seems like a mystical journey:

> *"I have to believe there was an original rhythm to my life, a spiritual road that I was traveling without ever knowing where it would lead."*[1]

~

When Michael was a child, his father James said he didn't suspect that his son would one day blossom into a sports superhero known around the world. "I had no idea all this would happen, and maybe that's better," James Jordan said. "If I had, I might've pushed him too hard and screwed him up. As it is, everything happened very naturally."[2]

~

Michael Jeffrey Jordan was born February 17, 1963, in Brooklyn, New York, where his father had moved temporarily to enroll in two years of vocational training on the veterans G.I. bill. Perhaps it isn't surprising that his parents named him Michael. The year he was born, the name Michael—meaning "he who is like God"—first topped the list as America's favorite name for boys, a position that it held right through the end of the century.

In hope of getting a better job, James, the son of a southern sharecropper, learned to build, repair, and service hydraulic equipment. Not long after the family returned to North Carolina, James landed a spot at a General Electric plant in Wilmington.[3]

When the family moved to Wilmington, they found a small, historic city, full of towering trees and azalea bushes. Wilmington stretches along the Cape Fear River at the point where it flows into the Atlantic Ocean. It is best known today as the location for filming *Dawson's Creek*, a nighttime soap opera popular with teenagers.

Michael's mother, Deloris, was a bank teller and later a customer relations representative at United Carolina Bank.

Michael was the fourth of the Jordan's five children. The oldest was James Ronald (Ronnie), followed by Delois, Larry, Michael, and Roslyn.

The Jordans tan and brick home on Gordon Road still attracts tourists, even though the family sold it and moved inland to Charlotte, North Carolina, in 1986.

∼

SURVIVING CHILDHOOD

Jordan and his parents look back and shudder at what might have been because of a series of mishaps Michael suffered as a child.

"There have been some very close calls in terms of my life."[4]

Deloris nearly miscarried while she was pregnant with Michael. When he was two, Michael received an electrical shock while playing with two extension cords outside in the rain-soaked yard. The jolt was severe enough to throw him backward.

Jordan's father said, "Michael was always . . . testing us. If we told him the stove was hot, don't touch, he'd touch it. If there was a wet-paint sign, he'd touch the paint to see if it was wet."[5]

WATER PHOBIA

Later in his childhood, water became Michael's nemesis. He nearly drowned at the age of seven at a Wilmington beach when he and a friend got caught in the undertow. The other boy drowned.

"I went swimming with a close friend one day, and we were out wading and riding the waves coming. The current was so strong it took him under, and he locked up on me. It's called the death lock, when they know they're in trouble and about to die. I almost had to break his hand. He was gonna take me with him."[6]

3

Five years later, Jordan was pulled gasping from a swimming pool while his baseball team celebrated their victory in a state championship. At the University of North Carolina, he was rescued again while trying to pass a mandatory swimming test. He had jumped in and tried to swim, knowing that he could not.

During his college years, his girlfriend tragically drowned after being pulled into flood waters that swept through Wilmington.

> *"I have a terrible phobia about the water. And I'm not embarrassed to say that. Everybody's afraid of something, so just don't ask me to go near any water."*[7]

SUSPENDED FROM SCHOOL

Deloris Jordan insisted that the children do chores, attend church, and go to bed early. Did the discipline include spanking? "'Why, of course!'" she says. "Mr. Jordan and I had to spank each of our children on numerous occasions."[8]

She recalled when Michael was suspended for three days in the eighth grade because he left the school campus to buy candy across the street. During the suspension, she took him to work and required him to do his classwork in her car, which was parked next to her office window. "He tells me now that that could be considered child abuse," said his mother. "But he never got suspended again."[9]

～

Jordan inherited none of his father's mechanical handiness. His father described him as a "lazy" teen, who disliked menial employment. To his parents' dismay, he quit one part-time motel maintenance job after only a week.

> *"One summer my mom said, 'You've just got to work,' and she got me a job as a maintenance man in a hotel. Man, I quit that job so quick! I just couldn't do it. I could not keep regular hours. It just wasn't me. From then on, I never, ever had another job."*[10]

～

Much of his success, Michael says, is due to his strong family background:

> *"My mother and father were such good parents that it made me want to be just like them."*[11]

～

Jordan was named to *Ebony* magazine's best-dressed list in February 1999, which isn't surprising. Michael's love of stylish clothes goes back to his childhood.

> *"When I was a kid, I always liked to dress up on Sundays."*[12]

～

"My children have made me proud because they are good human beings," says Deloris Jordan, "and as a parent, I didn't want anything more than that."[13]

Michael appreciates his mother's support:

"When it comes to dealing with any kind of problem I may have, she always has something positive to say, like 'Don't let it get you down,' and 'remember, we all love you.'"[14]

~

THE GIRLS WEREN'T INTERESTED

Michael earned fairly good grades in high school (he said he could have qualified for an academic scholarship) and successfully completed his college preparatory courses. He also took a home economics course, and surprised his family by baking an excellent cake.

"I took it because girls weren't interested in me, or whatever it was, and I thought, I may be alone for the rest of my life."[15]

~

Michael Jordan, the high-school wallflower, eventually would be named to *Playgirl* magazine's list of the 10 sexiest men in the world and *People* magazine's 1991 list of the 50 most beautiful people in the world. But he took up sports to be popular with girls.

"I was never very successful romantically. I was like the guy who carried their books home for them. I

was always the guy they wanted to be their friend, not their boyfriend. They always wanted the athletes."[16]

~

TWO MAGIC NUMBERS

Michael excelled at Pee Wee baseball, and played football as well. He learned a lot about basketball at home. His older brother, Larry, who also was athletic, competed with Michael both on the court and for their father's approval. One-on-one games with Larry helped Michael hone his competitive drive.

"Larry always used to beat me on the backyard court. His vertical jump is higher than mine. He's got the dunks and some 360s, and most all the same stuff I got. And he's 5-feet 7-inches! Larry is my inspiration."[17]

~

One of Jordan's most painful memories was being cut from the varsity basketball team his sophomore year. At 5-feet 10-inches, he was of only average height. He later recalled the shock of discovering that Leroy Smith, a sophomore friend who was taller than Jordan that year, made the team while Jordan had not.

"I went through the day numb. I sat through my classes. I had to wait until after school to go home. That's when I hurried to my house and I closed the

door of my room and I cried so hard. It was all I
wanted—to play on that team."[18]

"I saw the hurt," his mother recalled. "I told him to
go back and discipline himself. But I also told him if
he worked hard and still didn't achieve his goal, it just
wasn't meant to be."[19]

~

Although he played with the Laney High School
Buccaneers' varsity squad the next year, bitterness
over his varsity rejection lingered through his college
and early professional career.

*"It's something I've never forgotten. During my
first few years in the NBA, I would check into hotels
under the name Leroy Smith. That's the name I used
when we went to Los Angeles and won our first title.
Leroy Smith."*[20]

~

When Michael was a guest on America Online's CBS
Sportsline, one of the people who interviewed him
asked who had influenced him the most during his
basketball career:

*"It would probably be my high school basketball
coach [Clifton "Pop" Herring]. The one who cut me
from the varsity team. He would pick me up at 6 A.M.
for practice."*[21]

~

Jordan chose the number 45 for his high school junior varsity basketball jersey, but when he moved up to the varsity team his junior year, that number already was taken—by his brother Larry. Michael settled for number 23, because it was close to half of 45.

He used 23 throughout college and in the professional ranks though he reverted to 45 when he played minor league baseball with the Birmingham Barons and temporarily when he returned to the Chicago Bulls.

～

James Jordan once suggested that his son's greatness was always meant to be. "I've got to believe one thing. One day, God was sitting around and decided to make the perfect basketball player. He gave him a little hardship early to make him appreciate what he would earn in the end, and called him Michael Jordan."[22]

～

Michael seems to agree that a higher power gave his life direction:

"How can you say there isn't a plan for all of us?"[23]

NOTE: For more on MJ's sense of predestination, see the section "Zen and the Art of Basketball."

THE TAR HEEL

NORTH CAROLINA—THE RIGHT PLACE

When it was time for Michael Jordan to go to college, he was not recruited by the team he had favored since childhood, North Carolina State University. Jordan said:

> *"Growing up, I hated [University of] North Carolina. I was a State fan."*[1]

But when he was ready to go to college, it was neighboring South Carolina State University that aggressively recruited Michael, even inviting him to the governor's mansion in Columbia. Instead, Jordan settled on the University of North Carolina, home of the Tar Heels, a school that had been watching the talented young player.

Jordan insists the decision was not simply because the Tar Heel recruiters got to him early. In part, he was influenced by a visit to the UNC campus at Chapel Hill with a minority student program, Project Uplift.

"The coaches didn't know I was here. I saw this place as a student, not as a recruit."[2]

～

Jordan came to the attention of the University of North Carolina after his junior year of high school, when an assistant coach saw him play. First the assistants, then legendary head coach Dean Smith himself, watched Jordan during a basketball camp during that summer. He was recruited.

"We had decided that if we had been allowed only one player in the country, that player was going to be Michael Jordan," recalled Tar Heel assistant coach Roy Williams. "We worked hard to conceal it because he was not yet well known and we wanted to keep it that way. But it was also clear that he was the best player there. And we knew he was going to grow into that body and that he was just going to get better— how much better we did not know."[3]

NOTE: Michael's sister Roslyn skipped a grade in high school so she could start UNC-Chapel Hill the same year as her brother.

～

"Most people around Wilmington were predicting that if Michael went up to Chapel Hill, he wouldn't get to play," recalled Coach Smith. "[Michael] said, 'Coach Smith, I'm going to play up there.' And I said, 'Michael, that's why we're recruiting you. I think you will play.' And he said, 'I'm going to show them I can play.' I think he's shown a few people."[4]

~

As a freshman at North Carolina, Michael Jordan began to make a name for himself. His energy and talent soon drew attention, but he recognized that his game, particularly his defensive game, still needed work.

His team, including several stand-out players, was ranked number 1 in the country from his first varsity game, when the Tar Heels defeated Kansas. Jordan made 12 points in that game and told a reporter:

"I felt real comfortable out there. I felt good on my shots. I did throw a bad pass, though, and I need to help out more on defense."[5]

~

He played his way into the national consciousness March 29, 1982, when the Tar Heels defeated Georgetown 63–62 in the National Conference of Amateur Athletics (NCAA) title game. Jordan sank the winning 16-foot jump shot with 15 seconds left in the game.[6]

~

But in the fall of 1982, Jordan's sophomore year, the Tar Heels started the season against a string of strong opponents, tallying a lackluster 3–3 record in the first half-dozen games.

"Losing started to set in. I hated it. Questions pop into your mind, like when is losing going to end?"[7]

⁓

Nevertheless, North Carolina's record would have been worse had it not been for young Jordan's poise and finesse. He showed ability as a "closer," a player who can win games in the final moments. Against Tulane, Jordan picked up a loose ball and tossed it 24 feet to tie the score. The Tar Heels went on to win in triple overtime.

In another game, the Tar Heels turned on a powerful defense to defeat a Syracuse team ranked twelfth in the nation at the time. Jordan scored 18 points and made 7 rebounds, but he also showed flashes of defensive brilliance, blocking one jump shot from behind and leaping up to block and catch another opponent's jump shot in midair.

"He roams around like a madman, playing the whole court and causing all kinds of confusion," Maryland forward Mark Fothergill said.[8]

AN EIGHT-INCH ADVANTAGE

Not only was Michael Jordan displaying an instinct for the game, something remarkable had happened to him—he had grown from 5-feet 10-inches at the start of his sophomore year in high school to 6-feet 6-inches by the end of his sophomore year in college.

Coach Dean Smith recalled that when Jordan

returned from summer vacation between his fresh-man and sophomore years in college, "He hadn't been on any preseason All-America teams, but he'd grown two inches, had worked hard over the summer to improve his ball handling and shooting, and he had so much confidence."[9]

～

Jordan impressed the coach with his willingness to work harder than other players. After the Tar Heels lost their last game of the 1982–83 season to Georgia, Jordan showed up at Carmel Auditorium on the UNC campus the next day and practiced his shots for hours.

"I couldn't wait for my next game."[10]

During the next summer break, he played at the Pan American games and in less formal pickup scrimmages at home. When he returned to the campus, he quickly resumed his practices. Eager to test himself against the abilities of his new teammates, Jordan said:

"The freshmen were already talking trash. I had to see what they had."[11]

～

As a college junior, Jordan relished the prospect of taking on the stars of other teams, among them future National Basketball Association (NBA) players such as Houston's Hakeem Olajuwon and George-town's Patrick Ewing. Tough opponents challenged and motivated him.

"When I go against players who have gotten a lot of publicity, I always consider myself the lowest on the totem pole. That makes me work harder, because I want to get to the top."[12]

~

Jordan's loyalty to his alma mater held strong during his professional basketball career, and, whenever possible, he would watch North Carolina's televised games. In 1998, during his final NBA season, he watched an NCAA tournament that pitted his college team against North Carolina-Charlotte. When a UNC-Charlotte player tied the game in the closing seconds, a tense Jordan said, "I almost threw the TV out the window." His Tar Heels eventually prevailed in overtime, 93–83, but Jordan acknowledged he gets emotionally involved in North Carolina games.

"There [are] a lot of times I can't watch."[13]

~ ✳ ~

DEAN SMITH: THE VALUE OF A SUPERIOR COACH

When Dean Smith, legendary basketball coach of the University of North Carolina, was named *Sports Illustrated's* Sportsman of the Year for 1997, Michael Jordan, his most famous player, paid homage.

"He cared more for you as a person, and that transcended onto the basketball court."[14]

During Jordan's three years at UNC, Smith taught Jordan the fundamentals of the game, developing him into a well-rounded player, offensively and defensively. The lessons Smith taught served Jordan well throughout his career.

"A lot people say Dean Smith held me to under 20 points a game. Dean Smith gave me the knowledge to score 37 points a game and that's something people don't understand."[15]

Jordan was not the only college player to benefit from Smith's guidance. When Smith retired before the 1997–98 season, after 36 years at North Carolina, he had the best record of any college coach. His teams had won 879 games and lost 254. During his tenure, he took his teams to 23 consecutive NCAA consecutive tournaments. Of the players Smith coached, 26 became All-Americans.[16]

Dean Smith was born February 28, 1931, in Emporia, Kansas. His mother was a schoolteacher and his father a high school coach. Smith played football and basketball in high school, then went on to the University of Kansas on an academic scholarship and majored in math. On the powerful Jayhawks basketball team, Smith worked with a master, Jayhawks coach Phog Allen, who had learned his skills from James Naismith, the inventor of basketball.

Smith began his coaching career as an Air Force lieutenant stationed in Germany, where he coached the undefeated base basketball team. In 1955, Smith landed a job as assistant coach at the U.S. Air Force Academy.

He became an assistant coach at the University of North Carolina in 1958; three years later, when head coach Frank McGuire was dismissed, Smith was named his successor. Smith was so popular and respected that in 1981 he received a 20-year contract.

Smith's teams reached the NCAA finals in 1968, 1977, and again in 1981, but lost each time. Then came a freshman named Michael Jordan, who clinched the national title for the Tar Heels in 1982 with a basket in the final seconds.

Assistant coach Roy Williams recalled how Smith called time-out with 32 seconds left in that championship game. North Carolina trailed Georgetown by one point. Smith gave the team a confident pep talk. "Then he said, '*We* are going to determine who wins this game,'" Williams said. "And he grabbed Michael and said, 'Knock it down.'"[17]

Jordan kept in touch with Smith throughout his basketball career and even when Michael temporarily retired from the Bulls and took up baseball. In 1994, Jordan paid a surprise visit to his college coach's practice session, taking part in the scrimmage and advising Smith that the young players needed to work more on their defensive game.

Smith gave the players a situation: three minutes to play, with Jordan's blue team trailing by three points. Jordan's team won, as Jordan sank a jump shot with 10 seconds remaining.

Who was guarding Jordan? Smith replied, "Nobody apparently. We were trying to double him, but he still made the last shot."[18]

A DIFFICULT FAREWELL

A cultural geography major in college, Jordan was also good at math; he was sociable and struck his friends as having a special capacity for fun and happiness. He played pool, bicycled, or watched TV. He also played golf, which would become a passion later on. He and his college roommate, Buzz Peterson, dated a lot of different girls but avoided commitments.

"We felt like we were young and we still had a whole life ahead of us."[19]

Following his junior year in college, Jordan led the U.S. Olympic basketball team to a gold medal victory in Los Angeles; that fall, he was selected by the Chicago Bulls in the National Basketball Association draft. He said at the time about leaving college early:

"Leaving North Carolina was difficult because these have been the best three years of my life. It's time to move on to the next level and meet a new challenge."[20]

Michael was still young when he became a professional athlete, and his family continued to be a stabilizing influence. His mother moved to Chicago and lived with him during his rookie year. "I felt he needed a home environment," she said. "I wanted to make sure he kept his head on straight."[21]

Jordan often returned to Chapel Hill to visit his former coaches, men who had helped him grow into a responsible adult. On one occasion when he returned to watch his college team play, he arrived late, to find the parking lot full. A friend suggested that Jordan park in a handicapped space near the gymnasium. "Oh, no. I couldn't do that. If Coach Smith ever knew I had parked in a handicapped zone, he'd make me feel terrible—I wouldn't be able to face him."[22]

THE NBA'S LORD
OF THE HOOPS

HERE COMES MR. JORDAN

Michael Jordan's professional basketball career began June 19, 1984, when he became the third pick in the NBA draft, behind Hakeem Olajuwon, who went to the Houston Rockets, and Sam Bowie, who joined the Portland Trailblazers. It was a day of celebration for the Jordans. His mother and father left work early. A television station crew went to their Wilmington home, although Michael was in Indianapolis, practicing for the Olympic Games. "We had the biggest party ever in the neighborhood that night," said James Jordan.[1]

Looking back on his NBA drafting, Michael recalled:

> *"There had been some disagreements about whether the Bulls should take me, so when they picked me I was happy. I had never even been to Chicago. I didn't know anything about the city, nothing. I didn't know anything about the team except that it was bad. I didn't know any of the players, any of the*

past players, nothing. I didn't know much about the NBA at all."[2]

~

It didn't seem to bother Jordan to go from a top-ranked college team to the struggling Chicago Bulls, which had won only 27 of its 82 games the previous season:

"Chicago is a young team, and we have a lot of hard work ahead. The only way for the Bulls to go is up, and I'm really looking forward to making a contribution."[3]

~

Because of his college record and his performance at the 1984 Olympics, the Bulls had enormous expectations for Jordan. At the start of the season, the team took out advertisements in the local media, announcing his addition to the "cast" of a production called "Here Comes Mr. Jordan," It was a spin on the 1941 movie of the same name.

~

Indeed, Michael Jordan was a star before his first official NBA game, drawing crowds and reporters to his preseason matches. When the Bulls played the New York Knicks in Glen Falls, New York, the game drew 6,500 spectators. The town's population was 14,000.

"Michael is unbelievable," remarked Bulls guard Dirk Minniefield three weeks before the start of Jordan's first pro season. "Houston and Portland are both going to be sorry they didn't draft him. The thing is, he keeps getting better every day. If he keeps doing that, he'll be Superman. Wait, he already is Superman."[4]

NOTE: For more about the Superman image, see the section by that name.

BLUE IS FOR HEAVEN

For a player from a small city in the South, getting used to congested, heavily trafficked Chicago was a challenge. Jordan complained about the "wild drivers in this town."

"They ain't like that in North Carolina."[5]

To help himself make the transition, when he played basketball Jordan always wore his blue North Carolina shorts under his red Bulls uniform:

"You have to have some blue on somewhere. All this red stuff is the devil's colors. Blue is for heaven."[6]

Jordan wears another talisman, a tattoo:

"On my chest, I have an Omega sign. That's a horseshoe. It's for good luck."[7]

~

The Chicago Bulls beat the Washington Bullets 109–93 in Michael Jordan's debut in the NBA. Then coach Kevin Loughery said "Michael did not play that well" and seemed to have "first-night jitters."

But the coach said Jordan did a number of small things that helped the team as a whole. His presence was an instant psychological boost, helping to draw a large, noisy crowd of 13,913 for his first NBA game.[8]

∼

And that was only the beginning. The team's attendance nearly doubled during his first year, jumping from an average 6,365 a game to 12,763, and demand for tickets continued to increase. "Without Jordan, we could have lost 500 season tickets this year," Bulls ticket manager Joe O'Neil said.[9]

∼

Jordan seemed unrattled by the expectation that he would reverse the Bulls' sagging fortunes.

> *"At Carolina, I was in a controlled system, and a lot of the crowd was pleased with my play. So if I just play my natural game, I won't have any problem keeping the crowd pleased. This is the most relaxed time of my career. The games come so quickly that if you have a bad one, you can put the past behind you and get ready for the present."[10]*

∼

Indeed, Jordan was named the 1985 NBA Rookie of the Year, but even Jordan could not imagine how successful he would become:

> *"I'm happy to come in and do a lot better than most people expected. It's all been a lot of fun and I've got-*

ten a lot of enjoyment. Maybe I'll never have another season like this with all the hype and all the attention on my career."[11]

HIS AIRNESS

Jordan's soaring leaps, midair twists, flying slam-dunks, lightning speed, and power delighted fans. He seemed to break the bonds of gravity, if only for a few seconds. His feats earned him the nickname "Air" (which his agent David Falk coined for Jordan's Nike shoe line). Later, the moniker became "His Airness," to signify that Jordan was considered the high-flying royalty of the sport. The number 23 on his jersey was familiar to sports fans around the world.

～

At times, Jordan seemed amazed at his own acrobatics, saying,

> *"I've never had my vertical leap measured, but sometimes I think about how high I get up. I always spread my legs when I jump high, like on my Rock-a-baby, and it seems like I've opened a parachute, like, that slowly brings me back to the floor."[12]*

～

Jordan won the 1987 NBA All-Star slam-dunk competition with acrobatic leaps that made it seem as if he were flying:

"I never thought I could get that high. I could have kissed the rim. It's almost as if I was looking down at it."[13]

I LOVE THIS GAME LIKE A WIFE

Jordan's relations with Bulls chairman, Jerry Reinsdorf, and vice president for basketball operations, Jerry Krause, soured in 1986. They tried to keep Michael off the court longer than he felt necessary after he had broken the navicular tarsal bone in his left foot on October 29, 1985, in the third game of his second season with the Bulls. Jordan FOUND it impossible to stay away from the game. During a winter visit to his college team at Chapel Hill, Jordan started to practice again. Ignoring his doctors' fears that he might reinjure the foot, Michael returned to the Bulls and finished the season. As for management's objections:

"They haven't experienced the game of basketball like I have. I love it like a wife."[14]

~

To protect him, Reinsdorf and Krause devised a system to limit Jordan's playing time the rest of the season. Recalled Krause, "The thing that got Michael and me off on the wrong foot was that he thought I said to him, 'You're our property, and you'll do what we want you to do.' I don't remember ever saying it that way."[15]

Jordan told a reporter how the episode made him feel:

"I was a piece of meat to him. He felt he could control me, because I had so much value to him. But he didn't realize that I had value to myself. I was independent, and I understood what I was."[16]

"They were businessmen, not sportsmen, and they didn't have a true appreciation for the game."[17]

With Jordan playing only 18 games in the 1985–86 season, the Bulls suffered a 30–52 record.

Jordan and some of his teammates called Krause "Crumbs" because of the bits of doughnuts that sometimes clung to his suit. The nickname stuck, and in 1987, Jordan said,

"Crumbs and I, we keep our distance."[18]

WAITING FOR A CHAMPIONSHIP

Despite his skill and popularity with fans, during Jordan's first seven years as a professional, the Bulls failed to win the NBA championship.

"No one really felt that a scoring leader could lead their team to a championship. But I think the scoring

was a part of the team's situation or my responsibility to that team. It wasn't selfish."[19]

~

In 1990, the Chicago Bulls battled the Detroit Pistons in the Eastern Conference finals, playing well enough to force the series to a seventh game. Jordan was humiliated and angry when the team lost that game. He rushed out to the team bus afterwards.

> *"And I remember my father coming on the bus. And I'm in the back, yelling and screaming at him. And he's doing his best to calm me down and say, 'It's only a game. You'll be given another opportunity.'"[20]*

In a rematch the following year, the Bulls swept Detroit four straight to capture the Eastern Conference finals and, ultimately, the NBA championship against the Western Conference champions, the Los Angeles Lakers.

~

Jordan felt personally responsible for the Bulls' success or failure.

> *"I was the nucleus of the franchise when I came here, and we went through a process of going bad to good. I have a certain responsibility to this franchise and to the city of Chicago."[21]*

~

To overcome the strongest opponents, players had to discipline both body and mind, he said.

> *"We learned that it took a little bit more than just desire, that you had to put the work on the basketball court, the determination. We had to use our minds; mentally we had to out-think the other team."[22]*

~

As his NBA career evolved, Jordan himself developed, going from a wiry 6-foot 6-inch, 185-pound college hotshot to a more mature 215-pound player, with a heavier, more muscular upper body resulting from his self-imposed, rigorous weight-training program.

Watching clips from his rookie 1984–85 year on his sports video, "Come Fly with Me," Jordan told *Chicago Tribune* columnist Bob Greene that it was like viewing "baby pictures."

> *"I see a very young, very motivated, very egotistical person. I see a person who is trying to create an identity for himself. I see a person who is trying to energize a city, and is teaching himself to do it as he goes along."[23]*

JORDAN'S WORK ETHIC

Red Auerbach, who coached the Boston Celtics during its long dynasty, wished he could have had Michael Jordan on his team: "The thing I love about Jordan, the thing I've always loved, is that he works. He works, and he makes every single player on the floor with him better, every time he's on the floor. And he's a leader."[24]

～

"Michael had that rare capacity to be a genius who constantly wanted to upgrade his genius," said former Bulls assistant coach John Bach.[25]

～

"He went from being a frisky, spontaneous all-court player to being one of the best low-post offensive players in the game," said Joe Dumars who, like Jordan, played for the same team, the Detroit Pistons, his entire career. "Not to mention a master tactician. And through it all, of course, one of the greatest scoring machines basketball's ever seen."[26]

FOCUS ON THE FUNDAMENTALS

Michael Jordan's willingness to practice as hard as he played during games was legendary, a drive that remained undiminished by success and fame. But practice alone wasn't enough:

> *"You can practice shooting eight hours a day, but if your technique is wrong, then all you become is very good at shooting the wrong way. Get the fundamentals down and the level of everything you do will rise."*[27]

～

COMPETITIVE EDGE

Jordan's friendly, off-court demeanor could be misleading to opponents. Once a game began, he turned into a keenly focused competitor. And he competed at everything. His college roommate, Buzz Peterson, recalled Jordan getting so angry over losing a Monopoly game, that he threw game money at Peterson. "Basketball or anything," said Peterson, "Michael hates to lose. Play cards with him and you'll have to stay until he wins, if it takes all night."[28]

"It's personal with me. Mentally, I'm going to find a way to beat this guy."[29]

Jordan, too, acknowledged that as a junior in college, his drive to win imposed emotional demands on him.

"I have to be a man and accept losing, but it's very hard for me."[30]

Jordan scored 63 points, a playoff record, against the Boston Celtics on April 20, 1986, but the Celtics still won the game in double overtime. A keenly disappointed Jordan said afterward:

"Forget the record. I'd give all the points back if we could win."[31]

Yet, when another team's players excelled, or when Jordan had an off day, he rarely seemed demoralized.

If anything, it stoked his competitive fires, driving him to even better performances.

In 1993, LaBradford Smith of the Washington Bullets (renamed the Wizards in 1998) scored 37 points on Jordan in one of Chicago's home games. The next night, Jordan's teammate Scottie Pippen laid down the gauntlet: Jordan should get his revenge by scoring 37 points against the Bullets—in the first half. Taking up the challenge, Jordan scored 47 points in the first three quarters.

"I wasn't mad. I just took it personal. I wanted to redeem myself."[32]

For opponents, going up against Jordan was the ultimate challenge. Asked what guarding Jordan was like, Nick Anderson of the Orlando Magic replied, "Hell. You ever been to hell before? You don't want to go."[33]

For teams opposing the Bulls, the key to victory lay in shutting down Jordan's game. In the late 1980s, the Detroit Pistons developed a particularly effective set of defense strategies called the "Jordan Rules." The no-holds-barred, stop-Jordan-at-any-cost defense—practiced by the likes of Jordan's future teammate, Dennis Rodman—often sent Jordan crashing to the floor before he reached the basket. The coordinated assault was very frustrating to Jordan.

"It should be the easiest defense in the league to tear apart. But we haven't done it. It's worked. They've accomplished what they wanted to accomplish."[34]

Ths Bulls instituted assistant coach Tex Winter's triangle strategy, which still revolved around Jordan but gave his teammates more passing and scoring opportunities.

~

When things were going his way—which they usually were—Jordan enjoyed strutting his stuff. During a game in Salt Lake City against the Utah Jazz, a fan heckled Jordan for slam-dunking over a shorter (6-foot 1-inch) Utah player. "Hey, why don't you pick on somebody your own size," the fan shouted.

On the next play, Jordan breezed past a 6-foot 11-inch Utah player, Mel Turpin, and dunked the ball again. "Is he big enough?" Jordan asked the fan.[35]

STAYING MOTIVATED

Successful athletes often say they can't let themselves get complacent, and Jordan was no exception. Throughout his pro career, he looked for reasons to stay motivated. During the first game with then-new Chicago Bulls coach Doug Collins, Jordan told him, "Coach, I'm not going to let you lose your first game."[36] During that game, Jordan scored 50 points— 21 of them in the fourth quarter—to beat the New York Knicks 108–103.

～

"It's easier for me to get ready for a game on the road because you're expected to lose when you play away from home. That's a challenge for me right there and that perks up my competitive juices."[37]

～

Juaquin Hawkins, a player on the Long Beach State basketball team, had a chance to play a few pickup games with Jordan while Michael was in Los Angeles filming the movie *Space Jam*. Hawkins recalled telling Jordan at one of the impromptu games, "You're not going to score on me." Jordan replied, "They all say that," then proceeded to dismantle Hawkins's youthful arrogance with a flurry of baskets.[38]

IT TAKES A BIG HEART

"Heart is probably the biggest key to success in basketball at this level. There are a lot of players who pass through the NBA with the ability, but they don't have the heart or the intelligence to get the job done. That's the divider, always has been. Give me four guys of average ability with strong fundamentals and big hearts and I'll take my chance every time. Big games come down to those two things. The team that executes is usually the team that reaches inside for that little extra. I want those kinds of guys with me."[39]

～

After the third game in the 1998 NBA championship series, with the Chicago Bulls leading the Utah Jazz two games to one, Jordan, at age 35, was considered an older player. He told reporters:

> *"It proves to them [the doubters] and to a lot of people that the mental toughness and the heart is a lot stronger than some of the physical advantages that you may have. I've always said that and I've always believed it."*[40]

        ∾

> *"The desire is always going to be there. Because if the desire is not there, that means the love wasn't there."*[41]

TALKING TRASH

Trash talk, a macho ritual of verbal taunts and insults, is a Jordan trademark on court—and sometimes off. The running commentary is intended to either rattle the foe psychologically or get teammates to play harder:

> *"If you don't bring your level up to compete with me then I'm going to completely dominate you, and I'm going to talk trash to you and about you while I'm dominating. That's my way of getting my teammates to elevate their game."*[42]

        ∾

Steve Smith of the Atlanta Hawks drew the tough job of guarding Michael Jordan during the Eastern Conference semifinals in 1997. Smith found himself having to keep up with both Jordan's cunning moves and his trash talk.

After Jordan hit a jump shot over Smith, he told him, "A little late on that one, weren't you?" Smith returned fire when Jordan missed a shot, asking him on the way down court, "Is that all you got?"

"I enjoy playing against Steve," Jordan said later. "We have the same kind of personality out on the court. We like to exchange a few words out there, but we're careful not to cross the line."[43]

~

Sportswriter Rick Telander convinced Michael Jordan to do a little one-on-one with him for a Sportschannel TV roundtable program called *Sportswriters On TV*. The two took to the court, and the trash talk flew. Jordan told Telander after insulting his "pale legs":

"No wonder you're all writers. . . . You're terrible *athletes. You're frustrated athletes, that's what you are. All of you. You can't play. You can't do nothing. And you dream all day long."* [44]

~

Not all of Jordan's on-court patter is "trash." When former New York Knicks player Mark Jackson fouled Jordan as he dunked the ball, Jordan gave Jackson some on-court advice:

"Mark was telling me he was a fool for going after my dunk. I told him every leader of a team has to be

willing to help out his teammates. You have to do more than just win. Then I told him he has Rookie of the Year wrapped up, so don't worry about it."[45]

⁓

Jordan enjoyed the trash talk and humor of his good friend Charles Barkley of the Houston Rockets. Barkley is entertaining off the court as well:

"He never holds his tongue. Sometimes he says the things you want to say, but you don't have the courage to say."[46]

⁓

At times Jordan can intimidate with just a stare. When the Bulls defeated the New Jersey Nets 116–101 in the 1998 playoffs, with Jordan scoring 38 points, he glared repeatedly at Nets coach John Calipari. After the game, Jordan explained:

"I was really just looking at him, seeing how much energy he utilizes in coaching, try to pick up what he's saying, trying to see if his philosophy transfers to his players.

"It's pretty fascinating, really. I haven't played against a guy who runs up and down the court as much as he does, yells, and shows so much energy. I admire those players for being able to deal with it."[47]

Calipari, for his part, said, "I didn't stare back. There is one thing I would never do as a coach—say anything to Michael Jordan. Not one word."[48]

TEAMWORK: THE CHICAGO BULLS

Although Michael Jordan was the highest scorer in the NBA 10 times, he understood that he was one of five team members on the court. Without good teamwork, even a superstar couldn't carry the Chicago Bulls to an NBA championship.

"Talent wins games, but teamwork and intelligence win championships."[1]

~

Building a team requires the right attitude:

"It's a selfless process, and in our society sometimes it's hard to come to grips with filling a role instead of trying to be a superstar. There is a tendency to ignore or fail to respect all the parts that make the whole thing possible."[2]

~

"When you see that certain players or the team don't seem to be in a great rhythm, you apply your indi-

*viduality to that point, your skills and see if you can
kind of carry the team until we can all get back on
the same page."[3]*

TEAM LEADERSHIP

Coach Phil Jackson viewed the early Michael Jordan
as a "Michelangelo in baggy shorts," a stellar player
who, nevertheless, had not quite mastered the art of
team leadership.[4] Under Jackson's guidance, Jordan
began to see himself as a player with the ability to
influence others.

Jordan was sometimes brutally honest with his
teammates, hoping to improve the Bull's overall
strength. In 1988, the Bulls went to the second round
of the NBA playoffs for the first time in seven years
by beating the Cleveland Cavaliers three games to
two. But after the Bulls' loss in Game 4, Charles
Oakley, then still one of Jordan's teammates, complained that he was working hard, but the plays
weren't coming his way. Jordan explained to Oakley
that the problem was not the plays called by Bulls
coach Doug Collins. Oakley, he said, wasn't being
aggressive enough.

*"Doug is trying, and has been trying, to get us out
of just relying on me. Everybody has an equal
opportunity to score in this offense, but sometimes
the other guys aren't used to taking charge. We need
more of that."[5]*

~

Though Jordan could be supportive, if teammates failed him in the heat of the action, he would not sacrifice the game to make the other players feel good. He reserved the right to take over.

> *"You always must give these guys the opportunity to shine. But at the same time, my philosophy always has been if I'm going to go down, I want to go down shooting."*[6]

~

> *"We all had to suppress our egos for the system."*[7]

THE JEALOUSY FACTOR

Sometimes Michael Jordan's teammates had difficulty suppressing their egos in favor of his. He didn't win popularity points with the other Bulls when Jordan described them as his "supporting cast." Sportswriters further bruised egos by dubbing the team "Michael Jordan and the Jordanaires."

~

Jordan's popularity took another hit when, reportedly, he told teammates to keep the ball away from Bulls center Bill Cartwright during the last four minutes of games. In one game against the Detroit Pistons, Jordan failed to pass to Cartwright nine times. Horace Grant, the Bulls' power forward at the time, groused, "If we're going to do anything we've got to stop playing Michaelball."[8]

Jordan acknowledged later that he had been unhappy when the Bulls traded away his friend Charles Oakley in 1988 to bring in Cartwright, a veteran in the waning years of his playing career.

Later, Michael made amends to Cartwright and to management who arranged the trade with a tribute to Cartwright across a two-page spread of Jordan's coffee-table book, *For the Love of the Game: My Story*. A sprawling headline across the top of pages 40–41 read: "I was wrong about the Charles Oakley-Bill Cartwright trade in 1988." Across the bottom was written, "I loved having Charles on the team, but Bill made the difference."[9]

~

Jordan avoided the media after he was besieged by reporters questioning his 1993 gambling trip to an Atlantic City casino. His friend, Scotty Pippen, temporarily replaced him as the team spokesman. Jordan was startled to hear what Pippen said about a game in which Jordan scored 54 points and the Bulls overwhelmed the New York Knicks in a playoff game:

> *"He [Pippen] was talking about my game, and he said something like it's not that we don't want MJ to get points, but it makes it tough for others to get in the game and step up when they have to. Comments like these make you wonder how your*

*teammates really feel about you. I was always
conscious, even worried, about creating jealousy or
animosity. But you can't let that stand in the way
of winning or succeeding. You hear some of the different comments after a game like this and think,
do they really feel that way or are they just saying
that?"[10]*

~

Despite his hurt feelings, Jordan understood that
his teammates were in a difficult position. When he
won the 1987 and 1988 slam-dunk championships,
Michael divided the $12,500 purse with his fellow
players:

> *"I did it because my teammates had been so under-
> standing. There was a lack of animosity over all of
> the attention I got, and they had all been very car-
> ing. They had worked so hard, and I had gotten all
> of the publicity and credit."[11]*

JORDAN'S FAME SPILLS OVER

Many Bulls players recognized that their lives would
be changed because they were on Michael Jordan's
team. Noting that the Bulls suddenly needed police
escorts during the preseason of Jordan's rookie year,
Orlando Woolridge said, "It's like being on the Michael
Jackson Victory Tour. He's Michael, and we're the Jack-
sons."[12]

～

The Michael Jordan effect meant more than just fame: "Having him," explained teammate Steve Kerr, "means you've got the mental edge over every team you play, because he's the best. Even if you lose a game or are down in a game, you've got him on your side. You're always in the game. Until we lose or get knocked off, we will always have that."[13]

～

In the last years of his career, Jordan and the Bulls so dominated basketball that good players on other teams wondered whether they would ever win a championship. A few lucky ones joined the Bulls and got on the winning side. Trent Tucker, who played for several NBA teams before going to the Bulls in 1992, recalled how Jordan reassured him after the Bulls lost a game in 1997. "I'll never forget the time Michael and I were on the bus after we lost a tough game at the Forum in L.A. He said, 'We're going to get you that [championship] ring, Trent.' He gave me that chance, and I'll always appreciate that."[14]

DENNIS RODMAN'S BULLISH REBOUND

Dennis Rodman's tattoos, body piercings, and Technicolor hair made him the wild individualist of the league. The "Worm," as he's called, had dated Madonna. Later, he married actress Carmen Electra in Las Vegas, sought an annulment days later, then changed his mind and withdrew the petition. Even so, the marriage lasted only six months. A cross-dresser, the rough-and-tumble, gifted NBA star once confessed that he liked to play basketball with his fingernails painted pink. Rodman is an entertainer, but he also is an outstanding rebounder and defensive player, who won the rebounding title seven years consecutively.

From 1986 to 1992, Dennis played with the Detroit Pistons. Along with two championship rings with that team, Rodman earned a reputation as a tough, sometimes dirty, player. Later, he played for the San Antonio Spurs but didn't care much for the Texas town. He began to miss practices and occasionally refused to stand with his teammates during game time-outs. The Spurs wasted no time in deciding to trade him.

Before signing with the Chicago Bulls for the 1995–96 season, Bulls' management had to answer the question: Could they keep Rodman under control? And before the Bulls could decide, they also needed the approval of their two top players, Scottie Pippen and Michael Jordan. Pippen—who still bore a scar on his chin from when Rodman sent him sprawling in a past game—seemed apprehensive. But Jordan was not:

"I believe in giving the guy an opportunity to prove himself. Maybe he's a changed guy. Maybe he understands things better than you think he does.

I'm going into this situation with an open mind and not looking for a time bomb to burst."[15]

~

As a new Chicago Bull, Rodman said that although he admired Jordan's and Pippin's abilities, he was not in awe of the two. Nevertheless, he did seem to relish the attention he, Jordan, and Pippen attracted wherever they played. Outside the world of basketball, however, Rodman had little contact with his teammates.

"It doesn't mean I don't get along with Michael. We both have the same model Ferrari, so we've talked about that. And we talk about basketball. We all get along on the court, and that's where it matters."[16]

~

Coach Jackson tolerated Rodman's unusual lifestyle as long as it did not interfere with the game. Rodman recalled: "Whenever someone would ask Phil Jackson if anything I've done surprised him, he would always say, 'Yeah, it surprises me that he needs a special tool to take his pressurized earrings out.'"[17]

~

Although Rodman became a key player on the Bulls' last three championship teams, he occasionally suffered lapses.

Rodman was fined more than $200,000 and suspended for six games in 1996 because of a head-butting incident during a game against the New Jersey Nets.

Jordan was quoted in the *New York Times Magazine* as saying, "We have to corral this individual and get him more focused."[18]

~

During the 1997 NBA Finals, when the Bulls were playing the Utah Jazz in Salt Lake City, Rodman let loose with an epithet directed at members of the Church of Latter Day Saints (Mormons), Utah's pioneer and still dominant religion. Despite an apology, he was fined $50,000.

Bulls coach Phil Jackson no doubt offended LDS people even more when he explained afterward, "To Dennis, a Mormon may just be a nickname for someone from Utah. He may not know it's a religious cult or sect."[19]

~

After Rodman pulled down 29 rebounds in a December 1997–98 game against the Atlanta Hawks, Jordan said:

"Dennis has been doing his job. He has been giving us a lot of opportunities. You have to give him credit. He has come to play every night. He has given us a big lift."[20]

~

"Dennis is totally different. I never question his attire or his hygiene. I don't infringe on him. He has ways of expressing himself that I don't agree with, but that's Dennis, and we let it go. I would be

opposed to seeing him in makeup or a dress on the basketball court. And as far as him playing naked, I just hope I'm not on the court."[21]

~

Although Jordan often spoke up for Rodman, he could also sound like a stern father when Rodman's behavior threatened the Bulls' chances of winning. When Rodman started showing up late for practices after the coach did not put him in the starting lineup of a 1998 playoff game against the Indiana Pacers, Jordan complained at a press conference that:

> *"This is a crucial time of the season and the last thing we need is some B.S. from Dennis . . . We've always given him enough room to be Dennis. But when we come to work, he has to be here to work. I think that's something Phil [Jackson] wants to reiterate. If he needs our leadership, Scottie, myself, and the players will step in accordingly."[22]*

~

When the NBA lockout and labor dispute ended in 1999, Rodman was 37 years old. Like Jordan, he had decided to retire. But—as Jordan had done once in his career—Dennis changed his mind after a few days and signed with the Los Angeles Lakers. Wearing dark glasses and a large, flamboyant hat, he held a press conference to discuss his Lakers contract, which he said would earn him the NBA minimum (prorated to about $475,000 for the 1999 lockout-shortened season).

When a reporter asked him whether it had been selfish for him to drag out contract negotiations for three weeks, Rodman snapped: "I've been a team player, honey. I've been a team player for 13 years. I've got 5 championships, 7 rebound titles, I've been in the finals 10 years. For you to say something like that, you got problems. It's amazing, when Michael Jordan retired, he wasn't selfish. When Michael Jordan came back, you people right here kissed his . . . All of a sudden, I do something like this and I'm selfish. Another thing I want to put out there, I missed 10 games and I gave $1 million to charity. . ."[23]

Tears began rolling down Rodman's cheeks.

In fact Rodman's start with the Lakers was problematic. He missed a whole week of games when—with the coaches' permission—he went off to Las Vegas to gamble and sort out his personal problems. During his absence the Lakers often lost games; and though Dennis tended not to be friendly with other players, the team played more skillfully when he was on the court.[24]

When Rodman returned from his Las Vegas sojourn, he promised fans that he was back to stay. "I've used up my hall pass," he explained. "I have to get away. Kind of clear my head and make sure this is the right thing for me to come out and do. . . ."[25]

NOTE: Rodman was dismissed from the team a few weeks afterward for showing up late and without his shoes. He's now a professional wrestler.

Rodman was born May 13, 1961, and raised by a single mother in the Dallas, Texas, Oak Cliff projects. He played junior varsity basketball only briefly in high school; and, to his dismay, he was cut from the football team because he was too small. At high school graduation, Rodman was only 5-feet 9-inches tall, but like Jordan he went through a growth spurt. Two years later he was a towering 6-feet 7-inches.

After high school Rodman drifted for six months before getting a short-lived job as an airport janitor. He was arrested for stealing 50 watches from an airport shop, but managed to escape a jail sentence. As it turned out, he hadn't sold his loot; he had given it away. When police came calling, friends returned all of Rodman's stolen gifts.

Later, he played a semester for Cooke County Junior College, then dropped out of school. But coaches from Southeastern Oklahoma State University had spotted Rodman and offered him a scholarship.

"I figured I had to try again to get off those streets," Rodman said.[26] After an impressive college basketball career, Rodman was taken by the Detroit Pistons in the second round of the NBA draft in 1986. A late bloomer, he was already 25.

Although Rodman took a circuitous path to the NBA, basketball ability ran in the family. At 6-feet 3-inches, Debra, one of his two younger sisters, became an All-

American forward on Louisiana Tech's national championship-winning team. His other sister, Kim, 6-feet 1½-inches, also earned All-American basketball honors at Stephen F. Austin College.

SCOTTIE PIPPEN: BEAM ME UP, MICHAEL

Scottie Pippen said that when he came to the Bulls, the first words Jordan said to him were, "Oh, great, another country boy."[27] But over time the two developed a close kinship on and off the court, with Jordan playing the role of big brother.

After Jordan retired in 1993 to play baseball, Pippen influenced Michael to return to the Bulls. Jordan recalled talking to Pippen the season after he left: "I sat in the locker room and asked him how it was, how he felt, and he was suffering. He was taking the brunt of the (team's) rebuilding process, and he shouldn't have been. I could feel he wanted me back basketball-wise, and as a friend. And I missed him, too."[28]

∼

A Chicago Bull for 11 seasons, Pippen was the fifth chosen in the 1987 draft. Along with Jordan, he helped capture six NBA championships for the Bulls. He made the All-Star team seven times and was named to the All-Defensive team. After Jordan retired in 1999, Pippen joined the Houston Rockets.

∼

Born September 25, 1965, Scottie was the youngest of Preston and Ethel Pippen's 12 children. The family lived in Hamburg, Arkansas, a town of fewer than 3,400 people. Pippen's father worked in a paper mill until disabled by a stroke.

Like Jordan and Rodman, Pippen kept growing after high school, sprouting from 6-feet 1½-inches as a high school senior to 6-feet 8-inches during his college years.

Pippen needed a Basic Education Opportunity Grant in order to enroll at the University of Central Arkansas, where he studied industrial education and played basketball in obscurity, although brilliantly enough to attract the attention of Marty Blake, the NBA's director of scouting. "I advised as many teams as I could to go see him play," said Blake, "but when you're dealing with a player they've never heard of from a small college, the trick is to make people believe that he's bona fide. Some believe, and some don't."[29]

Jerry Krause, the Bulls' general manager and vice president of basketball operations, checked out Pippen and liked what he saw. Under a deal between Chicago and Seattle, the SuperSonics used their fifth draft pick to get Pippen and then traded him to the Bulls in exchange for Olden Polynice, whom the Bulls had picked up as the eighth choice in the draft.

Pippen's first contract with the Bulls reportedly totaled more than $5 million in salary and incentives for six years.[30]

Pippen recalled, "My first year or two, I admit that I messed around a lot. I partied, enjoyed my wealth, and didn't take basketball as seriously as I should have."[31]

But by 1991, Jordan saw Pippen steadily progressing:

"The main thing Scottie has to get is consistency. He has to reach the point where, if he has a bad game, people will just think it's a bad game, rather than think that he's an inconsistent player. He's almost at that point."[32]

Throughout his NBA career, Jordan went out of his way to share the spotlight with Pippen. When a *Sports Illustrated* reporter interviewed Jordan in the Bulls locker room, Jordan called Scottie over and talked up Pippen's skills, including his ability to dribble and dunk with his left hand.

"Who shoots threes better, you or me?" asked Jordan, conducting his own mini-interview.

Pippen hesitated. "You?"

"Nah, you do, no question," Jordan responded.[33]

In a *Sports Illustrated for Kids* profile, Pippen revealed that he was a good checkers player and owned two rottweilers. As a child, he said, he admired basketball star Julius Erving, poet Maya Angelou, and civil rights leader Martin Luther King Jr.

~

During the 1998 NBA championship series, Pippen was upset when the Bulls refused to renegotiate his contract, which, at the time, was worth $2.77 million. He expressed his desire to become a free agent, and as the Bulls dynasty wound down to an uncertain future, Jordan supported the decision:

> *"I think he's entitled to find out what his net worth is."[34]*

~

As the Bulls geared up for their sixth NBA title in 1998, Jordan said:

> *"I think Scottie is the reason, the major reason why we're here (in the finals). I think he's a unique and creative type of player offensively and defensively. And the harmony between the two of us is incomparable. And that's taken time to deliver, and trust each other to where we complement each other in the course of playing the game of basketball. I don't think you can start that over with anybody."[35]*

~

> *"Unfortunately, it may take a while, after we both retire, for people to realize just how good Scottie Pippen really was."[36]*

~

THE CHAMPIONSHIP SEASONS

Jordan won his first championship ring in 1991 in his seventh NBA season with the Bulls, then led his team back to the title the next two years. He retired, came back, and went on to help the Bulls win another three consecutive championships. Each victory was sweet, in its own way.

1990–91

After the final game of the championship series in June 1991, when the Bulls beat the Los Angeles Lakers 108–101, Jordan wept tears of joy.

"We started at the bottom. I never gave up hope. I always had faith. I don't know if I'll ever have this same feeling. What you see are the emotions of hard work. But this is a great time to be emotional."[37]

1991–92

One year later Jordan savored another victory, this time when the Bulls triumphed 97–93 in Game 6 over the Portland Trail Blazers. He said a second straight NBA title showed the Bulls were for real. But elation was tempered by his off-the-court difficulties, among them a sportswear licensing dispute with the NBA and controversy over a book, *The Jordan Rules*, which portrayed him as selfish to his teammates.

"I think all of my emotions were shown last year. This is a different kind of happiness. Especially with

*all that I've gone through, I'm just glad it's over and
done with."[38]*

~

The most memorable Jordan moment in the best-of-
seven finals for the second title came in Game 1, when
Jordan sank six three-pointers in the first half, helping
the Bulls to a 122–89 win over Portland.

> *"I was in a zone. My threes felt like free throws. I didn't
> know what I was doing, but they were going in."[39]*

1992–93

The next year also was stressful for Jordan. He was
accused of excessive gambling on golf and card games.
The NBA investigated Jordan, eventually clearing him
of violating league rules. But on the court he was the
same MJ. The Bulls defeated the Phoenix Suns 99–98
to win their third straight NBA championship, the
first team to do so since the Boston Celtics won eight
in a row in 1959–66. Jordan was named most valuable
player in the finals for the third year consecutively.

> *"Winning this championship is harder than anything
> I've ever done before in basketball, with all the ups and
> downs I've gone through this season and the mental
> approach that I've had to take into each game. We never
> gave up hope, and now that this team has become part
> of history, it's a very gratifying feeling for me."[40]*

1995–96

Jordan's fourth championship was more emotional than
the first. After his father's murder, Michael had retired

from basketball and detoured into baseball. When he made his comeback to basketball, some teammates, opponents, and the media suspected that he may be too old to compete at his former high level. But he proved them wrong when the Bulls seized their fourth championship, this time from the Seattle Sonics. Jordan was moved to tears—of joy for winning and of grief because his father wasn't at the game.

> *"I was blessed to be healthy throughout the season and blessed to be able to get the game ball of the championship game and bring a championship back to Chicago. It happened on Father's Day, which makes it even more special."*[41]

1996–97

One of Jordan's most legendary performances came during Game 5 of the 1997 NBA finals. Despite being so sick with a stomach ailment that he nearly passed out, Jordan rallied his team from 16 points behind and scored 38 points against the Utah Jazz. "I didn't even think he was going to be able to put his uniform on," said teammate Scottie Pippen, who had to help Jordan off the court after the game.[42]

Jordan said he felt he had no choice but to play, regardless of how ill he felt.

> *"If I give up, then they give up. No matter how sick or tired I was, I felt an obligation to the city and the team . . . I'm tired and I'm weak, but I have a whole summer to recuperate."*[43]

The Bulls went on to capture their fifth title in the next game.

1997-98

In the final seconds of Game 6 against the Utah Jazz, Jordan made a 17-foot jump to clinch a sixth NBA championship for the Bulls. Awaiting the outcome of the NBA lockout, he did not announce his retirement until the following year, but fans feared that they had seen Jordan's last hoop, a perfect arc of victory that would cap his career and symbolize his undiminished drive to win.

For the second time in his professional career, Jordan led his team to a "three-peat," three straight NBA titles.

"He's a real-life hero," said Bulls coach Phil Jackson.[44]

At what had become something of an annual celebration in Chicago, after the sixth victory, Jordan spoke nostalgically:

"I know a lot of people didn't think we would end up back in Grant Park [the championship rally site] this year. Nobody knows if we're going to be in Grant Park next year. But the one thing I do know is my heart, my soul and my love has always gone to the city of Chicago. And no matter what happens, my heart, my soul and my love will still be in the city of Chicago."[45]

Sadly, the 1997–98 championship was the "the last dance" for, arguably, basketball's most remarkable team. Coach Phil Jackson resigned from the Bulls soon after winning the title game. Later, Jordan would make good on his retirement threats. Scottie Pippen and other Bulls players became free agents the next season.

THE DREAM TEAM

Michael Jordan was a member of the first U.S. professional basketball team to participate in the Olympic Games, the so-called Dream Team of 1992. Because they were the titans of basketball, with little competition from other countries, media attention focused on practices that pitted Americans against Americans. Noted Jordan:

> *"I've been saying all along that only we can beat ourselves."*[46]

~

Scottie Pippen also played on the gold medal-winning 1992 team. As he prepared to participate in the 1996 Olympics, without Jordan on the team this time, he knew the experience would be different: "We were all NBA All-Stars and superstars," Pippen recalled, "and we played very hard against each other. I think our practices this summer will be just as good as they were in 1992. But they may not be quite as much fun because some of the veterans from 1992 won't be there. It's a different generation now."[47]

NOTE: For more on the original Olympic Dream Team, see the section entitled "Twelve Clint Eastwoods."

THE NEW CROP OF ROOKIES

Looking back on his career, Jordan counted himself lucky to join the NBA in the mid-1980s, a time when he had a chance to help excel at the game—and forge a unique image for himself.

The current crop of rookies, he said, were inheriting guidelines and expectations "and that makes it a lot harder for them because rather than being allowed to be themselves, they have to live up to certain expectations already predetermined."[48]

~

Jordan says that young players who skip part of their college years haven't fully developed their game. A lot of them aren't physically or mentally ready.

"A player who stays in college for four years is the player who's going to be good."[49]

NOTE: Jordan himself left college at the end of his junior year to join the NBA.

~

"For far too long, the owners have been paying these athletes on potential, and a lot of times it doesn't pan out. I think the owners just have to be more cautious about how they spend their money."[50]

~

And although Jordan set the standard for the marketing of an athlete, he still feels young players need to hold onto the values of the game. Being a strong role

model for them was one of his goals when he returned
to the Chicago Bulls in 1995.

> *"The young guys are not taking care of their respon-
> sibilities in terms of maintaining that love for the
> game and not let it get to where it's so business-
> oriented that the integrity of the game will be at
> stake."[51]*

ZEN AND THE ART OF BASKETBALL

COACH PHIL JACKSON

Between 1985 and 1989, a series of coaches—Kevin Loughery, Stan Albeck, and Doug Collins—came and went from the Chicago Bulls. Then Phil Jackson took over and the transformation of the Bulls began.

Under Jackson's leadership, the Bulls integrated veteran assistant coach Tex Winter's potent strategy—the triangle offense—into their play. The crux of the strategy was that it moved attention away from a single player to the entire team. Jackson improved team harmony and successfully melded players of different styles and talents.

The strategy worked, and the team soon embarked on a long stream of championship seasons.

~

By the time he joined the Bulls, Jackson had a long and personal relationship with the game of basketball. He had attended the University of North Dakota on a basketball scholarship and was a two-time All-American.

After graduating from college in 1967, he was drafted by the New York Knicks, which won two NBA championships during Jackson's 11 years on the team.

His career had entered a transitional phase when he became player-coach for the New Jersey Nets. After an interlude as television sports commentator, he spent four years with the minor-league Continental Basketball Association (CBA). He joined the Bulls in 1987 as an assistant coach, and when head coach Doug Collins left in 1989, Jackson stepped up.

Jackson was respected for his knowledge of the game and his analytical ability, but what distinguished him from other coaches is his intellectual power and his emphasis on spirituality.

MEDITATION

A Montana native whose parents were Pentecostal ministers, Jackson calls himself a Zen Christian. He drew from Native American religions and Zen Buddhism to help guide the team. He asked his players to meditate to help them clear their minds and create team unity.

Initially, Jordan was skeptical about meditation, opening one eye during the Bulls' first session to see whether teammates were taking the exercise seriously. Most were, even though Jordan would argue that he didn't need to meditate.

Jackson seemed to agree that Jordan could achieve a Zen state on his own: "In the process of becoming a great athlete," Jackson said, "Michael had attained a quality of mind few Zen students ever achieve. His ability to stay relaxed and intensely focused in the midst of chaos is unsurpassed. He loves being in the center of a storm. While everyone else is spinning madly out of control, he moves effortlessly across the floor, enveloped by a great stillness."[1]

~

Jordan has acknowledged that his desire to enjoy the moment was part of the Zen philosophy espoused by Coach Jackson.

> *"Yes, that's the theme of Zen Buddhism, and I think we have all taken some of that with us in some respects. Not all of it. I mean, Phil is way out there, and we're somewhere closer to Earth, a little bit, but certain things you take, and you can evaluate, and associate it with you personally. 'Living in the moment' is something that I will continue to always understand and associate with my life."[2]*

VISUALIZATION

> *"When I do envision a big game, I usually go out and play passively at the beginning. I let the game come to me. It's very important that I don't go try to make it happen."[3]*

"When he fails, he doesn't dwell on the failure part of it," Phil Jackson observed. "He visualizes himself doing it successfully the next time."[4]

LIVING IN THE MOMENT

After his sixth NBA championship game, during which he scored 45 points, Michael discussed the Zen state that helped him excel.

"The moment starts to become the moment for me. And that's part of that Zen Buddhism stuff. Once you get in the moment, you know you're there. Things start to move slowly, you start to see the court very well. You start reading what the defense is trying to do. And I saw that, I saw that moment."[5]

"Physically, I prepare myself. I'm geared for everything. Each time I step on the basketball court, I never know what will happen. I live for the moment. I play for the moment."[6]

In 1998, Jordan had a chance to win a game against the Utah Jazz—and the NBA championship—with 1.1 seconds to go. The Jazz deflected one inbound pass, and with less than a second remaining, Jordan missed a final shot. The Jazz won by two points.

Far from worrying about the loss, which proved a temporary obstacle on the path to a Bulls championship, Jordan turned philosophical after the game. He talked about games that came down to one final play, where for an instant, fans were left in suspense. He relished the uncertainty.

"No one knew what was going to happen. Me, you, no one who was watching the game. And that was the cute part about it. And I love those moments. Great players thrive on that in some respects because they have an opportunity to decide happiness and sadness. That's what you live for. That's the fun part about it."[7]

WINNING THROUGH INNER PEACE

"The basketball court is still my refuge; even when the season ends, it's the place that I can go and find answers. It's like I can go talk to the game because I know it's going to give me a response. I've done that my entire life."[8]

～

"When I step onto the court, I don't have to think about anything. If I have a problem off the court, I find that after I play, my mind is clearer and I can come up with a better solution. It's like therapy. It relaxes me and allows me to solve problems."[9]

～

During the stressful 1998 finals, Jordan relaxed by playing a piano in his hotel room, although he confessed that he was just learning how to play. "I just push the keys."[10]

～

To reporters covering the 1998 best-of-seven finals, Jordan seemed both calm and intense.

> *"Instead of being frustrated, I just want to smile and let it flow. Just channel my thoughts, my frustration, in a whole different form. And I feel good about our chances, and I feel confident. And I kind of forced myself to say, 'Hey, I'm going to enjoy this moment, it may not happen again.' This may be the last time, the last dance, whatever. Maybe I was taking it too seriously, and I should enjoy it. And that's my mood from now on."[11]*

～

Coach Jackson said Jordan had only rarely exhibited anger, even in the face of on-court provocation. "In my mind, Michael is the epitome of the peaceful warrior," said the man who coached Jordan during his championship years.[12]

PREDESTINATION

After his father was murdered in 1993, and Jordan briefly switched careers to baseball, Jordan said he wasn't worried about the risky career move because:

> *"...someone has already planned which way I will make them. So it's not really my decision after all."[13]*

JORDAN'S DARKEST HOURS

The first five years of the 1990s were difficult for Michael Jordan, starting with accusations that his gambling was out of control, followed by the brutal murder of Jordan's father, and ending with a less-than-grand side trip into professional baseball. Jordan, though, turned it into a period of personal growth and maturation. When it was over, he returned to basketball to give his fans some of the most thrilling moments of his career.

GAMBLING: A COMPETITION PROBLEM

Michael Jordan likes to gamble, likes to play golf, and likes to bet on his golf games. These proclivities might have remained a secret pleasure had Jordan not found himself entangled in a murky chain of events that ended with the murder of one golf partner and with another golfing friend prosecuted on drug and money-laundering charges.

When these matters first became public, Jordan told reporters:

> *"I have a right to associate with whomever I choose."*[1]

And indeed, when the allegations were investigated by the National Basketball Association, he was cleared of gambling violations in the spring of 1992.

∼

Jordan explained he could not be compared to Pete Rose, the baseball player who was found guilty of betting on his own sport of baseball.

> *"I can safely say this is not like the Pete Rose matter. I wasn't involved in any point-shaving or betting on basketball games."*[2]

∼

Even so, Jordan later sounded contrite:

> *"My mistake came with the people I was involved with, not really knowing of their associations. A lot of the information I [later] received about the people was very shocking."*[3]

Jordan's troubles began in 1991, when Jordan played golf at a posh resort on Hilton Head Island, South Carolina, where he has a vacation home. Among the golfers was James "Slim" Bouler, a pro shop owner from Monroe, North Carolina, who, unbeknownst to Jordan, in 1986 had been convicted of selling cocaine.

Jordan lost $57,000 to Bouler gambling on golf and card games, and paid the full amount with a cashier's check. Bouler, as it turned out, was under surveillance, and in December 1991, federal authorities seized his property, among which they found Jordan's $57,000 check.

In a taped phone conversation, Bouler told an unidentified associate he hoped to avoid paying taxes on his gambling winnings by saying the money was a loan. When the case was first publicized in 1991, Bouler said Jordan lent him the money to develop a golf driving range. Jordan countered, "It's a loan. I've known [Bouler] for four or five years."[4]

~

Bouler was indicted in 1992 and tried in the Charlotte, North Carolina, federal court in October of that year. By then, Jordan, under oath, did not support Bouler's driving range story.

During nine minutes of testimony at Bouler's trial, Jordan acknowledged that he gave Bouler a $57,000 cashier's check "for what I lost gambling on golf and later in poker when he loaned me some money. I didn't have any money [at the time]."[5] On the stand, Jordan acknowledged, "It was not represented as a loan at all."[6]

Under cross-examination in court, Jordan explained his original remarks to reporters:

"It was my immediate reaction to the media, after a game, to save embarrassment and pain . . . and the connection to gambling."[7]

~

When Bouler took the stand, he said he was the one who suggested representing the $57,000 as a loan. "I told him [Jordan] there probably would be a lot of nosy people asking about it," Bouler said. "I told him if they ask me, I'll tell them it was a loan."[8]

~

The federal jury acquitted Bouler on a charge of possessing cocaine with intent to distribute but convicted him on four counts related to money laundering.[9] Bouler was sentenced to nine years.

~

On February 19, 1992—only 13 days after Bouler was indicted—another of Jordan's golf partners, Eddie Dow, a Gastonia, North Carolina, bail bondsman, was murdered in front of his home.

Dow's attorney, Stephen Gheen, found photocopies of three checks, totaling $108,000, among Dow's personal effects. The checks were either signed by Michael Jordan or drawn from his ProServ management account. Police said the checks were unrelated to Dow's murder. (Three of Dow's former employees and another man were arrested.)

Gheen said Jordan and Dow had been friends and

that at least part of the money was Jordan's repayment of gambling losses.

New York Times columnist Dave Anderson speculated that Jordan was set up: "Without knowing the valid handicaps of Dow, Chapman or any of the others, it's unfair to wonder whether Jordan got hustled. But even on the up and up, anybody with a golf ego as large as Jordan's, especially with a bank account to match, is always an easy mark if he's not as good as he thinks."[10]

~

In May 1993, as the Bulls played in the NBA championship for the third straight year, allegations surfaced in the *New York Times* that Jordan had been seen at 2:30 A.M. in an Atlantic City casino, following the Bulls' loss of Game 2 of a Round 1 playoff series to the New York Knicks.[11]

Jordan angrily sparred with the media at a news conference, admitting that he went to the casino but insisting he was back in his New York City hotel room by 1:00 A.M.

> *"I chose to take a ride in a limo, didn't drive, rested, sat there talking about all the different conversa-tions my father and friends could talk about, got up there, gambled in a private area, and was home by a respectable hour. That's the truth. Whoever saw me there at 2:30, whatever, I would like to see them in person because I'd certainly lay a lawsuit on them."[12]*

~

Jordan contended that the media unfairly was making him look irresponsible to his team. Accustomed to positive press, the media attention on his personal life troubled him. Jordan decided to stop speaking to reporters.[13]

His father, James, shouldered the blame, insisting he had encouraged his son to go the casino to relax before the next game. He denied that his son had a gambling problem, telling reporters, "He wouldn't be doing it if he couldn't afford it. He's not that stupid. He's got a competition problem. He was born with that. If he didn't have a competition problem, you guys wouldn't be writing about him."[14]

FALSE FRIENDS

In June 1993, businessman Richard Esquinas, former president of the San Diego Sports Arena, revealed he was about to self-publish a book titled *Michael and Me, Our Gambling Addiction, My Cry for Help*, alleging that both he and Michael Jordan were compulsive gamblers. Esquinas wrote that when the two played golf, Jordan ran up gambling debts of up to $1.25 million. Jordan, he said, won back enough to reduce the debt to $902,000. Esquinas claimed the amount was negotiated down to $300,000. (Esquinas reported receiving two checks of $100,000 each from Jordan's financial managers.)

NOTE: Jordan says Esquinas exaggerated the amount of the gambling debt.

The Esquinas book outraged Jordan. He broke his self-imposed media boycott to issue a statement, offering an apology and an explanation so that "this sensationalized report" would not hurt his team's chances of defending its championship.

> *"I have played golf with Richard Esquinas with wagers made between us. Because I did not keep records, I cannot verify how much I won or lost. I can assure you that the level of our wagers was substantially less than the preposterous amounts that have been reported.*
>
> *"It is extremely disappointing to me that an individual whom I caused no harm and who held himself out as my friend would shamelessly exploit my name for selfish gain. It is equally disappointing that my off-the-court activities are receiving more attention in the midst of the NBA championship than my on-court activities.*
>
> *"I want to publicly apologize to my family, my teammates, Jerry Reinsdorf, the NBA and Bulls fans for the distraction this story has caused. I also want to thank those members of the media who had the courage and independence to report this incident and the coverage it received for what it is: an embarrassment for all of us."[15]*

Still, Jordan denied having a gambling problem. In June 1993, he said:

"I want to reestablish that I don't have a problem and that I'm in control of my life financially, emotionally, and physically, and I felt the reports were kind of misleading in that sense."[16]

The same month, he told sportscaster Ahmad Rashad that his family had not expressed concern over his gambling.

"They never came to me and said, 'Michael, you have a gambling problem.' My wife never said anything, and she's the chief of finances in our household."[17]

~

The NBA assigned former federal judge Frederick Lacey to investigate Jordan's gambling on two occasions. The 1992 probe ended with Jordan's being cleared of wrongdoing. The second investigation a year later was closed two days after Jordan announced his retirement. NBA commissioner David Stern announced there was "absolutely no evidence Jordan violated league rules."[18]

~

While Jordan's on-court athletics were breathtaking, many of his friends and basketball colleagues poked fun at his golf game. New Jersey Nets power forward, Jayson Williams, joked that if he joined the Chicago Bulls, he could make his money off-court at Jordan's expense: "I figure I'll take Michael out on the golf course, beat his brains in, and make the money that way."[19]

~

"Have I ever been surprised by anything Michael does?" joked his friend and opponent Charles Barkley. "Yeah, I've been surprised a couple times. When he missed a putt for $100,000. That's it."[20]

~

For Jordan, the gambling episodes were painful learning experiences.

> *"I'm not allowed to make mistakes. You make a mistake and it's magnified. It makes you scared to live your life."[21]*

~

> *"My shell is hardening with each mistake, and it should. It's hard to trust people now . . . No one said it was going to be all roses, but I would never change my lifestyle or things I've gone through because I think they've made me a better person."[22]*

~

After the gambling controversies, Jordan lamented to reporters:

> *"No one's perfect. Michael Jordan, you, or anyone else. I think the lesson that comes from this is that when you make a mistake, you've got to stand up and accept it and move on."[23]*

THE MURDER OF JAMES JORDAN

The tragic murder in 1993 of Michael Jordan's 56-year-old father, James—Pops, as he was called affectionately by Bulls team members—left Jordan reeling with grief, gasping at the specter of random violence. He also had to face the shock that his own generosity might have contributed to his father's death.

James Jordan was returning to his North Carolina home from the funeral of a former coworker when, in the middle of the night, he pulled his red Lexus 400 off U.S. 74 to take a nap. The expensive car was a gift from Michael. He was shot in the chest with a .38-caliber pistol by two 18-year-old car-jackers who robbed him, then dumped his body and took a joy ride before abandoning the car.

Daniel Andre Green (who later changed his name to Lord Danielle As-Saddiq Al-Amin Sallam U'Allah) and Larry Martin Demery were arrested August 15, 1993, and later convicted of the murder. In 1996, both were sentenced to life in prison.

$\sim$

James Jordan's family had not been particularly concerned when he didn't arrive home on schedule. He was known as something of a free spirit. But eventually they did begin worry. It would be several weeks before they learned how and why he had been killed.

James Jordan's body was discovered August 3 in Gum Swamp on the North Carolina–South Carolina border. His car was discovered, stripped, outside Fayetteville, North Carolina, on August 5. His body, as yet unidentified, was cremated before family members could confirm that it was James; but on August 13, he was identified by dental records.

Although Deloris Jordan waited to file a missing person report until the day after her husband's car was discovered, the family was worried, according to Wayne Lofton, a bail bondsman and private investigator. "Michael had his security people out looking for his father long before anyone knew anything was wrong, but they wanted to keep it private," said Lofton, a longtime friend of the Jordans. "They did not want to cause any alarm or attract a lot of press coverage.

"The family suspected something was wrong. Even though he [James] was often out of touch for long periods of time while traveling on business, he always talked to at least one of them. When no one heard from [him], they became concerned."[24]

∿

Reporters were not permitted to attend Jordan's funeral at the Rockfish African Methodist Episcopal Church in Teachey, North Carolina.

Lofton, who attended the service, said Michael read a eulogy. "He talked about his dad's life and how they meant everything to each other. He said his father made him what he is . . . the kind of man he is, the kind of athlete he is. His father was his partner."[25]

∿

In his first public statement after his father's death, issued through his agent David Falk, Jordan thanked the public for its outpouring of sympathy and the police for their investigation.

> *"When James Jordan was murdered, I lost my dad. I also lost my best friend. I am trying to deal with the overwhelming feelings of loss and grief in a way that would make my dad proud."*[26]

~

> *"One thing about my father's death, it pointed out that life can be taken from you at any time."*[27]

TERRIFYING ALLEGATIONS

Jordan was angered that some reports initially linked his father's death to allegations about the basketball star's gambling. His father's sportswear businesses also came under financial scrutiny. (James Jordan and other family members owned and operated JVL Enterprises in Rock Hill, South Carolina, and Flight 23 by Jordan stores in Charlotte, North Carolina.[28])

Later, it became clear that the crime was random and unrelated to any of Michael's or his father's activities. According to their confessions, the youngsters who killed James Jordan were looking for unsuspecting tourists to rob that night and happened upon Jordan, sleeping with his car window down.

Michael Jordan noted that most reporters had

approached the story with "dignity, sensitivity, and respect for human decency," but he added a few engaged in baseless speculation:

> *"I simply cannot comprehend how others could intentionally pour salt in my open wound by insinuating that the faults and mistakes in my life are in some way connected by my father's death."*[29]

~

Once published, Jordan pointed out, unfounded speculation is hard to undo:

> *"When some people don't know the true facts, they speculate, which gives a false assumption. But whenever they do find out the truth, they can never give those things back to the person."*[30]

~

During Green's trial, his partner Demery said the two planned to steal James Jordan's car but had not intended to kill him. "I don't know if he [James Jordan] had heard us," Demery testified, "but he sat up and kind of made a statement like 'What's this? What's going on?' As soon as those words came out, Daniel cut him off. What I mean by that is Daniel shot him."[31]

~

The murderers, described by authorities as highway robbers, stupidly made a video after the crime, which was confiscated by police in the trailer Green occupied with his mother. In the video, the two were dancing to rap music. Demery wore James Jordan's Air Nike golf shoes and Green flaunted two rings and a watch Michael had given his father. Michael identified the rings that he had given his father— his 1986 All-Star game ring and a replica of Jordan's first NBA championship ring—from still photos and videos supplied by the police. Michael also identified a replica of his 1991–92 NBA championship watch with the inscription, "To Dad, Love Michael and Juanita."[32]

~

Michael Jordan did not attend the murder trial.

"The damage has been done. Justice may prevail, but there's no justice when there's no life."[33]

GRIEF CATCHES UP

Grief caught up with Jordan on a rainy day during a road trip with his minor league baseball team, the Birmingham Barons. He recalled that he was in his hotel room watching a Wesley Snipes movie that ended with the death of the main character's father.

"The room was dark, and I was lying on the bed, and I guess it hit the right buttons because all of a sudden, I couldn't stop crying. I talked to my wife. I called everyone I knew. And I still couldn't stop crying."[34]

~

"It's been one big mythscape for Jordan ever since his father's murder," wrote Mark Jacobson in a 1997 *Esquire* article. "A sweet little classic structure it is, too: The father creates the son, enables him on the path to unimagined greatness and wealth, and then is killed because he's driving the showy car given him by his rich son. But it is Jordan's near-bodhisattva display of compassion that arrests the heart and mind. Saying, 'For me to have anger and frustration and anger continuously for the rest of my life because of what one individual has taken away from me really doesn't give me an opportunity to live my life for my kids, who will follow in my footsteps,' Jordan eschewed vengeance, instead choosing to renounce his supreme art to humble himself as a commonplace minor-league baseball player."[35]

~

In 1996, Deloris Jordan spoke of how her grief-stricken family had pulled together:

"There is a void. The children have lost a father who has always been there, and I have lost a husband. But there are just some things you can't control. So we pick up the pieces, bond closer together, and talk more."[36]

~

Michael tried to view his father's violent death in the most favorable light possible.

"Some children never have their fathers for any years, and I had mine for almost thirty-one. No one can convince me that I was unlucky."[37]

~

Though he tried to take a positive perspective on events, after the murder of his father, Jordan grew wary of danger. He began carrying a pistol for protection and had the security tightened at his children's school.

"I'd love it if there were no danger, no guns, a society that doesn't kill needlessly. But we don't live in that society. I always hoped we would, but we don't."[38]

~

In October 1994, the Chicago Bulls and the Charita-Bulls, the team's charity arm, announced a donation of $4 million to build a 60,000 square-foot, state-of-the-art youth center, to be called the James Jordan Boys and Girls Club.

"What we are trying to show is appreciation for a man who has more or less given me everything that you see—every talent, every personality. What the James Jordan Boys and Girls Club will do is give the kids who may not have had that positive influence the opportunity to make their way out of the ghetto and maybe into a much richer and positive life for themselves and their family."[39]

THE FIRST RETIREMENT

When Jordan retired in October 1993, he told reporters he was glad that his father had seen his last basketball game, when the Bulls captured the 1992–93 NBA championship. But he insisted his father's murder was not the reason he was quitting basketball.

> *"His death didn't alter my decision one way or the other. I had already made up my mind at that point . . . Naturally, when my father died, it put a little bit different emphasis on life."*[40]

~

Though Jordan still believes his grief did not affect his decision to retire early, he later explained:

> *"When I said I was going to retire, this was a low point in my life. I was looking for answers."*[41]

~

Knowing that even the best professional basketball players move on at a young age, Jordan had mulled life after retirement since his college days.

As a student majoring in geography, he wanted to be a college professor when his basketball career ended. He later dreamed of becoming a professional golfer, telling *Sports Illustrated*:

> *"I'm not saying I'm going to win. I'm gonna try, but I'd just like to make it out there, to be competing with these guys on the tour."*[42]

When he revealed to Phil Jackson his plans to leave the game, his coach tried to persuade him to take a sabbatical instead. But finally Jackson had to accept Michael's decision.

"It was so tough. I had never seen Phil cry. And he was very genuine about it. I never saw the emotional sides of a lot of the guys until it was time for me to leave."[43]

His ten NBA seasons had left Jordan mentally exhausted.

"My breaks were not really vacations. It was just a time-out."[44]

Some 300 members of the media gathered at the Sheri L. Berto Center, the Chicago Bulls practice facility in Deerfield, Illinois, October 6, 1993, to hear Michael Jordan's retirement announcement. He joked:

"This is probably the first time I've met this many people without a scandal around."[45]

Then Jordan got serious, saying he had nothing left to prove in basketball.

"I've always stressed to the people who know me . . . that when I lose the sense of motivation as a basket-

ball player, then it's time for me to move away. I'm very solid on my decision not to play [basketball]."[46]

~

Jordan did not immediately tell the public that he had other plans in professional sports:

"I'm going to watch the grass grow and then go cut it."[47]

NEVER SAY NEVER

Although Jordan stunned the sports world, and particularly Chicago fans, when he announced his retirement in 1993, he left them with room for hope of a comeback.

"I'm not going to close that door. I don't believe in the word 'never.'"[48]

~

A number of athletes who had retired in their prime predicted correctly that Jordan would take a breather from basketball, then return. Former Washington Redskins quarterback Joe Theismann said, "Michael says he's heard the cheers and won't miss it, but I don't believe it. That's why you play the game. You miss the performance. After I was out for two years, I wanted to play so bad. You want to play for pure personal gratification and satisfaction.

"I think that's why he'd go back. We've been athletes for so long that we don't know anything else. If he can stay away, I'd consider it a monumental feat."[49]

A DETOUR INTO BASEBALL

Jordan rocked the sports world a second time in one year by announcing his decision to pursue a lifelong dream. He signed a minor-league contract with the Chicago White Sox on February 7, 1994. He noted that his father had always wanted him to play baseball.

"I'm ready for it. I'm not afraid to fail. I'm a strong enough person to accept failure. But I'm not going to accept not trying."[50]

Questions swirled: Was Jordan earning a chance at pro baseball on his athletic skills, or was it because of his connections? After all, Jerry Reinsdorf was chairman and co-owner of both the Chicago Bulls and the White Sox.

Perhaps to dispel notions that marketing potential rather than athletic ability motivated the contract, Jordan demonstrated his baseball skills to the crowd of reporters gathered at the Illinois Institute of Technology. Though he caught fly balls and ground balls, reporters observed that his batting fell short of big-league standards. Jordan agreed:

"Speed and defense will be my strong points, but hitting is something I have to adjust to."[51]

～

Jordan himself seemed uncertain about how well he would do as a major league baseball player. He told reporters that he had approached Reinsdorf and White Sox General Manager Ron Schueler.

"I told them, 'If this is a hoax, let me know. Be a friend first.' But they have an eye for the game, and they've given me some confidence."[52]

～

Before going to the Double-A Birmingham Barons in March 1994, Jordan worked out with the White Sox at their spring training camp in Sarasota. "He was out at 6:30 each morning hitting with [batting coach] Walt Hriniak," said White Sox spokesman Scott Reifert. "It would be different if he acted like he was a big shot or had it made. But there wasn't anybody here who put in more time and worked harder."[53]

Jordan's presence at spring training camp drew hundreds of reporters from around the world and sent sales of White Sox memorabilia soaring. Reifert said his most vivid memory was of a line of pro ball players waiting for Jordan's autograph. "Now that was a strange sight."[54]

～

As a member of the Birmingham Barons, a White Sox farm team, Jordan's pay was less than $2,000 a month, which included his meal allowance—a pittance compared to his basketball salary.

"It isn't for the money. It's just the idea of trying to see if I can do this. I have a lot to prove, to my friends and family—and certainly to my [late] father, who I know is still watching me. That's a good driving force."[55]

~

"If anybody didn't think I was serious, it was because they could not see the blood dripping off my hands or those 6:00 A.M. batting sessions."[56]

~

Jordan's batting average was an unimpressive .202 during his first season. But he showed promise, stealing 30 bases and driving in 51 runs.

At his own request at the end of the regulation season, he was permitted to play fall season baseball games with the Scottsdale, Arizona, Scorpions. To prepare, he returned to Ed Smith Stadium, the White Sox spring training facility, to practice.

At the end of his first baseball season, Jordan reflected:

"I went through a lot of stages very quickly. I had some success. I had some down times. Overall, I think I've come a long way."[57]

~

Jordan played in the Arizona Fall League with the Scottsdale Scorpions in late 1994. Improving his batting, he hit .252 in 35 games.

It became apparent that despite his athletic ability, Jordan was at a disadvantage. He hadn't played baseball since high school 12 years earlier. Terry Francona, Jordan's manager on the Barons and, later, the manager of the Philadelphia Phillies, said Jordan might have succeeded "if he had played another couple of years of baseball, if he had maybe 1,000 at-bats [in the minors].

"One thing I would never do is tell him, 'No, you couldn't make it.' One thing you never tell Michael is 'You can't do something,'" said Francona.[58]

~

Some of Jordan's friends couldn't resist teasing Jordan about his baseball dreams. When Jordan attended a basketball game between his alma mater, North Carolina, and Maryland, he ran into Rick Brewer, the Tar Heels' sports information director and asked him, "Why are you still here?" Brewer good-humoredly shot back, "I don't have to retire. I can hit a curve ball."[59]

A STRIKE SENDS HIM OUT

Jordan was scheduled to move on to the Triple-A Nashville Sounders in April 1995, on a track he hoped would lead to his entry in the major leagues. But a baseball strike was an unforeseen obstacle he couldn't overcome. The strike had brought an abrupt halt to major league games during the previous season, and now had filtered down to the minor leagues.

Though Jordan was a friend of Jerry Reinsdorf, co-owner of the Chicago White Sox, and was grateful for the chance Reinsdorf had given him to play baseball, he also hoped to join the Major League Baseball Players' Association. Months before, Jordan made it clear he would not continue playing in the minors if the team owners tried to break the strike by using replacement players from the minors during the 1995 season.

When Jordan showed up in Sarasota for spring training, the strike was still on. He decided he did not want to be used to boost attendance at exhibition games using replacement players. So after leaving the practice field March 2, a frustrated and disappointed Jordan issued a statement saying the strike prevented him from developing his skills.

"As a result, after considerable thought and with sadness and disappointment, I have decided to end my [baseball] career."[60]

"I didn't want to see it [the strike] happen, just like any fan, but I accept it as a business situation. I think the focus on the strike will project a negative image in the fans' thinking. But I think fans understand that sport is business and you'll have confrontations as you would in any business. The game will not be tarnished as much as most people think."[61]

The *Chicago Tribune*'s Paul Sullivan reported that the day before Jordan left the Sarasota training camp, he saw Jordan crumple a piece of the paper and land it perfectly in a trash can at the other end of the clubhouse. Jordan said:

"I still have the touch."[62]

The day he departed from Sarasota to return to Chicago, Jordan asked the pilot of his private plane to fly over the practice field and dip a wing. The White Sox players below waved good-bye.[63]

∽

After Jordan left baseball, he said that in some ways, he never truly abandoned basketball.

"When I was down in the minors, every guy wanted to play me in basketball. I used to play on Sundays with some of the guys in Arizona. We'd go and rent a gym and play pickup games. And I think these guys thought I'm retired or maybe they're like me, they think they can be a basketball player just as much as I think I can be a baseball player. But really, each time I played, my appetite got a little bit greater."[64]

∽

Though the outcome probably wasn't what he would have liked it to be, Jordan took away good memories from his baseball experience.

"The camaraderie is different, especially inside the clubhouse. Baseball players tend to hang around the clubhouse more. They tend to spend a lot more time together and go out together a little more. Baseball players are more group-oriented. Basketball players tend to break out in twos and threes and go their separate ways. I love the camaraderie here [in baseball]."[65]

THE LONG BUS RIDES WERE GOOD FOR JORDAN

In hindsight, Jordan felt he made the right decision to try baseball, recalling his need to get away from the NBA and sort things out during "the long bus rides and staying in low-budget motels and trying to make it to the big leagues."[66]

～

"Going through baseball gave me the chance to revisit those levels of hard work and determination that I seemed to have forgotten or came quite easy over a period of time. Now I give my dedication to shooting before the game or in workouts and improving my overall skills, sharpening my tools. It [baseball] was my time to evaluate my dedication to the game of basketball. Without baseball, I don't think I would have come to that conclusion."[67]

～

The controversies and media criticism that dogged Jordan during the early 1990s angered him then, but Jordan says he came to accept it as part of the baggage of fame.

> *"I knew people were going to start taking shots at me. You get to a point where people are going to get tired of seeing you on a pedestal, all clean and polished. They say, let's see if there's any dirt around this person."*[68]

~

In his postbaseball years, Jordan remained an avid major league fan, rooting for the Atlanta Braves in the 1995 World Series. Commenting on Atlanta's long quest for the championship, Jordan said:

> *"I don't want to see anybody spend their whole lives as a bridesmaid. That's why I hope Charles Barkley [his good friend] wins the NBA title—after I retire."*[69]

THE NBA COMEBACK

Children around the world were among the fans most eagerly hoping for Jordan's return to pro basketball. Weeks before Jordan abandoned his baseball quest, his basketball comeback had been forecast by Long Island, New York, middle school students. Published in *Newsday*, Roger Zienkowicz, a student from Mastic Beach, wrote, "Bulls need him. Dad visits him as an angel, tells him to join the Bulls."

Michael Gerusimov of Commack Middle School wrote: "Michael Jordan: He will leave baseball and go back to basketball."

There was one dissenter. Ariel Ronneburger, a Packard Middle School student, gave a subtle double-message in her prediction. "Michael Jordan: Nike Air Pump sneakers are inflated too much. Takes off never to be seen again."[1]

In early 1995, widespread rumors began circulating that Jordan would return to the NBA—and to a

Chicago Bulls team struggling without him. The prospect titillated the sports world. Reporters swarmed the Bulls' offices, awaiting word of his homecoming. President Clinton hinted at a Jordan reappearance, when he announced that the economy had generated 6.1 million jobs since he took office and "if Michael Jordan goes back to the Bulls, it will be 6,100,001 new jobs."[2]

~

The rumor mill generated a story that Jordan's foray into baseball was merely a cover for a secret NBA suspension he supposedly received for his gambling excesses. Days before Jordan announced his return to professional basketball, NBA Commissioner David Stern scotched those rumors, saying, "People had us having this talk in my living room. But it categorically never happened. My position on Michael is this: 'Tell him we've left a light on for him, and to come on in. We're Motel 6.'"[3]

~

When Jordan finally made his return official, the announcement was a simple, "I'm back."

A HERO'S WELCOME

Jordan seemed stunned by the outburst of public euphoria and blatant hero worship accompanying his return to the Bulls. He said:

"I was shocked with the level of intensity my coming back to the game created. It was embarrassing. It's great to be respected, but not great to be praised. People were praising me like I was a religious cult or something. That was very embarrassing. I'm a human being like everyone else, but I was being treated like I'm superhuman."[4]

~

Chicago Bulls coach Phil Jackson explained the public outpouring: "To many, Michael is the prototype of a hero, the Sir Galahad riding to the rescue, and it's elevated him to such high proportions, a Prince Charming, a storybook character, one of those things people carry in their hearts and their hopes."[5]

~

When asked why he ever left basketball in the first place, Jordan said:

"I think at the time I walked away from it, I probably needed it—mentally more so than anything. But I really, truly missed the game. I missed my friends. I missed my teammates. I missed the atmosphere a little bit. So I was eager to get back into the little things."[6]

~

"I'm still in the same mode of trying to win championships, and at the same time, I'm trying to have fun, too. Everything is fun. I played for fun for nine straight years. We happened to win championships."[7]

~

"I'm under the same contract. There's nothing under the table. I wish there were. I'm strictly back for the love of the game."[8]

BUT DOES HE STILL HAVE THE TOUCH?

After he returned to basketball, Jordan said:

"I want to be on top. Now, I'm not there, but I know what it takes to get there, and I want to work my way back up."[9]

~

"I have an individual drive and I have a team drive. As long as I'm playing, I set high [standards], and I want to live up to them."[10]

~

Although Michael Jordan was an active athlete during his hiatus from basketball, he noted that baseball and basketball require different conditioning. Switching back to basketball forced him to work hard to return to top form.

"I don't think people truly understand the difference. From fingertips to forearms, baseball players have an unbelievable amount of strength. Basketball is about fluency of strength."[11]

~

In 1996, the Chicago Bulls defeated the Los Angeles Lakers in a game billed as a rematch between the Lakers' Earvin "Magic" Johnson, who also had come out of retirement, and Jordan, already well on his way back to top form. Afterward, Jordan had encouraging words for Johnson, who scored 15 points in the game.

> *"We [he and Johnson] may not be as physically gifted as we once were, but we're more knowledgeable. What you saw was as much as we wanted to play. There are other players on the court contributing. [The Bulls] had a good supporting cast. He may not have had the same. I don't have any doubt he can come back and be the kind of player he wants to be."[12]*

~

Dennis Rodman was not as kind, saying that Johnson would have to "work his butt off" to compete against players the calibre of Rodman, adding that "he [Magic] doesn't have the legs for that now."

Furthermore, Rodman gave both teams much of the credit for the quality of the game: "It's not just the Magic Johnson and Michael Jordan show. Players came off the bench and did a great job."[13]

RETURN TO TRIUMPH

Jordan showed flashes of his former brilliance in a matter of a few games after his return to the NBA. In his fifth game, he scored 55 points, leading his team to a 113—111 victory over the New York Knicks. Jordan took his performance in stride:

"I knew I wasn't that far away. I guess it took four games to really get my rhythm down. I was nervous it was going to take longer."[14]

~

After that Knicks game, when a reporter asked whether he could keep playing at that level, Jordan replied:

"I don't know. That's the fun thing about it. Tomorrow, you don't know what I will do."[15]

~

In 1995, with Jordan back on the team, the Chicago Bulls made the NBA playoffs only to be knocked out of contention by the Orlando Magic. Publicly, Jordan said he was not discouraged, expressing no regrets over his decision to come out of retirement.

"Every year is not going to be a great year, but I hope to be able to do what's necessary to make Chicago a champion again. We're not that far away."[16]

~

But Jordan confided to friend and filmmaker Spike Lee, an avid Knicks fan who had worked with Jordan on a Nike commercial series in the 1980s, that he had been unprepared.

> *"I thought I could live off my reputation and the game proved me wrong. The game taught me the lesson. It wasn't Orlando that taught me, or New York. You can't leave and think you can come back and dominate this game. I will be physically and mentally prepared from now on. I promised myself that."*[17]

~

Jordan gave himself a challenge. After an off-season of intense training, he sounded confident again:

> *"I'm sure people are going to be critical of Michael Jordan's game. I realize that. I look forward to the opportunity to prove. That's part of my energy and determination."*[18]

NOTE: The rejuvenated Jordan and the Bulls amassed a 72–10 record for the 1995–96 season and went on to win the NBA title, the first of three consecutive championships.

~

In the 1996 All-Star game in San Antonio, Texas, the first for Jordan since coming out of retirement, he led the East team to a 129–118 victory over the West.

He was named most valuable player, over Shaquille O'Neal, whom many in the crowd believed should have won it.

"I felt kind of strange standing out there with the MVP trophy and the crowd making their own selection. I wish I could have done something about it. But I don't vote. It's one of those circumstances I can't control. If it's going to make him [O'Neal] mad the second half of the season, he can take it. I don't have a problem with that. I'll be glad to give it to him when I get back in the locker room."[19]

Despite the MVP incident, Jordan was pleased with his All-Star performance.

"I always thought I could play basketball. I never doubted that. I just wanted to come back and have a good time. I hadn't experienced this in a few years. And as I looked at a lot of players I could see myself and some of the nervousness, the expectations. I relived a lot of the memories. In retrospect, [coming back] was a fantastic accomplishment for me."[20]

Jordan said his daring but difficult comeback taught him important lessons:

"If you do the work, you get rewarded. There are no shortcuts in life."[21]

~

Sam Smith, a Chicago sportswriter often critical of Jordan, said of the star's 1995 return to the NBA: "He came back a changed man. He stopped feeling sorry for himself. He embraced the media. Magic was gone. Larry Bird was gone. He had the basketball stage completely to himself. And he likes that. He likes the spotlight."[22]

REVOLUTIONIZING THE SPORTS ECONOMY

Filmmaker and devoted basketball fan Spike Lee described Michael Jordan as having the "total game, the total flawless package, and he's the best promoted and most marketable athlete since Babe Ruth."[1]

~

Business Week proclaimed that Jordan was "more than a basketball star. As marketers say, he's a power brand—a player whose popularity and reach is peerless in the history of sports business."[2]

~

The 1984 Olympics gave Jordan worldwide publicity, but he attributes his global popularity to the "regular guy" image corporate sponsors promoted off the basketball court. What was created was a sales package that transformed a sports hero into a marketing machine:

"What changed the game to some extent and what really propelled me to where the kids can relate with me was the marketing of an athlete."[3]

~

The influence Michael Jordan came to have on sports fashion should have been apparent early on. When he joined the NBA in 1984, Jordan wore baggier and longer shorts than other players so that he could wear his lucky North Carolina shorts under his Bulls uniform. By the end of his thirteenth NBA season, even players not wearing lucky college shorts under their regulation uniforms were following his style. Today, basketball shorts are 7 to 10 inches longer than in the mid-1980s.[4]

NIKE: JORDAN AND THE GODDESS OF VICTORY

The union between Nike athletic shoes and a young NBA rookie named Michael Jordan would become the defining example of the mutual benefits that could be reaped from a relationship between business and athletes.

When Jordan signed up with Nike (named for the Greek goddess of victory), the upstart athletic shoe company headquartered in Beaverton, Oregon, was in a slump. The company, which made its name initially with its running shoes, was slow to see the magnitude of the aerobic exercise movement, and as a result, had lost considerable market share to its rival, Reebok.[5]

Michael Jordan reversed Nike's fortunes, when in 1985, the league began fining Jordan for wearing his trademarked red-and-black Nikes, which didn't conform with the Bulls' uniforms. Nike paid the fines, which ranged from $1,000 to $5,000 a game. The company made a commercial featuring his Nike shoes, stamped "banned."

Jordan said:

"It would have cost millions of dollars to come up with a promotion that produced as much publicity as the league's ban did."[6]

Initial sales of Michael's signature product, called Air Jordans, reached $110 million, and Philip Knight, Nike's Stanford-educated chief executive officer, drew nearer to his goal of creating a powerful global sports company.

Nike's revenues rose from $877 million in 1987 to $3.4 billion five years later. The company's stock went from $1 a share in 1984 to $11.31 a share in October 1993, when Jordan first retired, to $42 a share in January 1999, when he retired for the second time.[7]

～

Some of Jordan's early Nike commercials were done with the young, still unknown, filmmaker, Spike Lee, whose movie, *She's Gotta Have It*, was a quirky little story about a character who idolized Michael Jordan.

Spike Lee created the *She's Gotta Have It* character Mars Blackmon the same year Air Jordans hit the market. The pairing of Mars and Michael in a commercial appealed to Lee when it was proposed by Nike's Portland-based ad agency. But would Michael buy into the idea?

Lee recalled, "Jordan had no idea who I was at the time, had not seen the movie, and could have easily decided to say, nah, let's get a hotshot Madison Avenue director, but he gave me a break. If Michael had said he wanted the next man instead, that would have been it for me, but Jordan decided to give a young brother a chance. I'm still in his debt for saying yes."[8]

~

The first commercial aired in 1988 and featured Lee as his movie character, Mars Blackmon, wearing black-and-red Air Jordans and ruminating about Michael Jordan's magnificent "hang time."

TWELVE CLINT EASTWOODS

When Jordan and the other members of the original U.S. basketball Dream Team won an Olympic gold medal in Barcelona in 1992, they wrestled with the problem of having to wear ceremonial uniforms by Reebok when many had contractual ties with other sports shoe and apparel companies. At the medals ceremony, they turned their Reebok-marked collars under. Jordan, Charles Barkley, and Magic Johnson also draped U.S. flags over the company's logo.

Jordan explained:

> *"They're going to have to learn that when they send 12 Clint Eastwoods over to do a job, they can't ask what bullets they're going to use. The only way I could think of [to hide the manufacturer's name] was the American flag. I didn't want to deface the uniform, and I knew the American flag wouldn't deface anything."*[9]

Jordan voluntarily demonstrated his loyalty to Nike at the Olympics. Nike's CEO told Jordan that the company would not consider it a contract violation to wear the Reebok-made uniform for the medals ceremony.

> *"But Phil didn't realize how loyal I really am. I think I surprised him."*[10]

After the Olympics, Jordan said he regretted participating in the Olympics because of the dispute over corporate logos. He had agreed to play because he didn't want to generate negative publicity.

> *"I would have been called un-American and unpatriotic. That wasn't true, because I played in the '84 Olympics. But my family would have had to read about it. I could take it, but my wife hates it, my*

mother hates it, the whole family hates it when people are so critical of me."[11]

~

By 1993, Jordan began to worry about the personal impact of his corporate image.

"Nike has done such a good job of promoting me that I've turned into a dream. In some ways it's taken me away from the game and turned me into an entertainer. To a lot of people, I'm just a person who stars in commercials."[12]

ADVERTISING THE FAILURES

Among Jordan's favorite Nike ads was one that aired in 1997. It shows him missing shots and losing games. In it he says:

"I've missed more than 9,000 shots. I've lost almost 300 games. Twenty-six times, I've been trusted to take the game-winning shot, and missed."[13]

He thought it was important to demonstrate that he had to overcome failures in order to succeed.

Jordan said that his agency had resisted the idea of an ad focusing on imperfections, preferring to have him develop a commercial with movie director Oliver Stone.

"And I said, 'Oliver Stone don't know shit about basketball. Why don't you just show the actual situa-

tion? Let the people see exactly what's happened over the 12 years of my career?"[14]

～

Jordan did more than make commercials for Nike. He promoted his trademarked products in everyday life and made a point of noticing when people weren't wearing his brand. During a 1987 visit to Pittsburgh to promote Coca-Cola, Jordan agreed to a television interview, joking to a camera operator to be sure that the camera picked up the Nike logo on his T-shirt. He told the interviewer:

> *"It's a habit of mine now, noticing labels, logos, shoes. For instance, your sound man, with his Fila jacket and his Reeboks . . . I haven't said anything to him yet, but I will."[15]*

～

During Jordan's temporary detour into baseball, Nike used the sports star in two commercials, one of which made light of his baseball experience. Nike spokesman Tom Feuer explained that, "whether he is in basketball or baseball, Michael is a cultural icon and we would be foolish not to use him as much as we can."[16]

The 1995 Nike ad showed Spike Lee complaining that Jordan did not measure up to baseball legends Willie Mays, Stan Musial, or Ken Griffey. The three major league baseball stars retorted, "He's trying."

In the second of those commercials, Jordan's baseball effort was defended by Bill Buckner, a Boston

Red Sox first baseman who had missed a ground ball in the tenth inning of a 1986 World Series game. Boston ultimately lost the game—and the series—to the New York Mets. The commercial poked fun at Buckner's mistake, showing him missing a ball while filmmaker Spike Lee said, "Michael's no Bill Buckner." Buckner replied, "But he's trying."

When the commercial stirred up bad feelings instead of laughs among touchy Boston fans, Jordan issued a statement in Buckner's defense:

> *"We must understand, and fans must understand, that this guy was still a good player—he's a great player—and we should not just remember him for one bad play that he encountered."*[17]

THE DOONESBURY CARTOONS

Jordan was forced to consider the social consequences of Nike's third-world manufacturing facilities when critics said Asian women and children were producing the Jordan brand (among others) athletic shoes in sweatshops at very low wages. In Indonesia, Nike workers earned an average $117 per month, about the price of a single pair of the shoes they were producing. Even worse conditions came to light in Vietnam, where it was revealed that 30,000 to 35,000 women worked 12-hour shifts to make Nike shoes.[18]

Kathie Lee Gifford, whose own line of fashion clothing was revealed to have sweatshop connections, tried to enlist Michael Jordan to help her eradicate such workforce abuse. Said Jordan:

> *"I hear that Kathie Lee has kind of put me and other people in her fight or whatever. But I think that's Nike's decision to do what they can to make sure everything is correctly done. I don't know the complete situation. Why should I? I'm trying to do my job. Hopefully, Nike will do the right thing, whatever that might be."*[19]

The following year on *ABC Primetime Live*, Jordan explained his reticence on the sweatshop issue:

> *"I couldn't voice an opinion until I found out exactly what was happening and how that affected me."*[20]

He added that he was satisfied with a Nike study indicating the workers were paid fair wages.

Nike hired Andrew Young, the civil rights leader and former United Nations ambassador, to report on Asian conditions, but Young's credibility was undermined because he used Nike translators when he visited the factories. Doonesbury cartoonist Garry Trudeau spoofed the mistake. In one strip, Asian workers complaining about horrible conditions in their native language had their words mistranslated, claiming instead they were happy campers thankful for their wonderful workplace.

Trudeau revisited the issue in 1999, with a character asking: "Mr. Jordan, now that you've retired and have a little more free time, will you be honoring your public commitment to journey to Vietnam to investigate labor conditions in Nike shoe factories?" The cartoon Jordan replied, "Yeah, right," and broke up laughing.[21]

VIOLENCE OVER JORDAN PRODUCTS

Though the basketball star frequently expressed pride in the success of his line of Nike sports apparel, he was distressed over reports that, in poor neighborhoods, children had been robbed—occasionally, even murdered—for sneakers or jackets having the Jordan and/or the Chicago Bulls logos.

Jordan instructed parents to tell their children that if robbers demanded an item of their sportswear, they should hand it over. If the parents couldn't afford to buy another jacket or pair of sneakers:

> "They should say that I'll buy a replacement. . . . Why place your life in danger for a piece of cloth? The piece of cloth can be replaced. The child can't. I know that's not a message parents this has happened to are going to be helped by hearing. But parents have got to make their children understand that the clothing is just not that important."[22]

THE JORDAN BRAND

In November 1997, Jordan launched the Jordan brand, his own line of athletic shoes and clothing, operating as a subdivision of Nike. Jordan said:

> *"I have been involved in the design of everything I have worn from Nike since we began our relationship in 1984. The launch of the Jordan brand is simply an extension of that process. It is an exciting and challenging opportunity to express myself and connect with the next generation of players."*[23]

His first line of Jordan brand shoes featured the Air Jordan XIII, a lightweight style inspired by one of Jordan's nicknames, "Black Cat." The shoes cost from $90 to $150 a pair.

~

After Jordan's 1999 retirement announcement, Nike founder and CEO Phil Knight said, "He's grown from being a 21-year-old novice to becoming a very solid businessman and father. I'm happy to say that his retirement from basketball gives him more time to spend with the Jordan brand, and I would personally hope to spend more time with him in the future. I have no doubt that CEO Jordan is a step that he can make very simply."[24]

~

THE FALK FACTOR

David Falk, Jordan's longtime agent, was among the first to recognize Jordan's corporate potential. He was instrumental in helping Jordan line up numerous endorsement deals.

Although Jordan preferred Adidas sneakers when he entered the NBA, Falk arranged for him to meet with Nike, though his parents had to talk Michael into going to the meeting because he was very resistant. Later, Falk would be credited with thinking up the Air Jordan name.

In the mid-80s, Falk was a senior vice president of ProServ Inc., a sports marketing firm highly successful at promoting endorsements from a new breed of athlete pitchmen. Besides Nike, his early corporate deals included Chevrolet and Coca-Cola. The demand for Jordan's endorsement services mushroomed.

Asked if too many endorsement commitments would distract Jordan from the game of basketball, Falk replied, "If endorsements begin to interfere with Michael Jordan's ability to perform on the court, the endorsements will go away."[25] Jordan's game continued to improve despite a full schedule of endorsement contracts.

Falk left ProServ in 1992 to form his own company, and Jordan stayed with him. Jordan's loyalty drew other NBA stars to Falk's new endeavor, and smoothed the path for their corporate contracts.

Falk told *Sporting News* in 1997, "Working for Michael Jordan enables us to call the chairmen of

Nike, AT&T, WorldCom, Quaker Oats, Coke, and Pepsi. Michael creates tremendous opportunities and creates access for our clients."[26]

∼

Falk disagreed with pundits who contended Michael Jordan's image was a corporate fabrication. "No one ever tried to invent Michael Jordan," Falk said. "We didn't try to create something in 1984; it just evolved. When you try to create that, the public sees through it and they think it's insincere."[27]

∼

Before signing an endorsement contract with Wheaties, Jordan was asked by a company representative whether he actually ate Wheaties. Michael answered honestly.

> *"I could have easily lied. But I thought, why lie? So I told them the truth. I told them I had never eaten Wheaties and that I didn't know whether I'd even like Wheaties. I mean, we used to eat some kind of wheat puffs when I was growing up. They came in a huge bag. I don't even know if they had a brand name. We had five kids in the family. We couldn't afford Wheaties."[28]*

∼

By the end of his thirteenth NBA season, Jordan had corporate ties to a broad array of companies, including Nike, Bijan, Coke, General Mills (Wheaties),

Upper Deck, McDonald's, Wilson, Sara Lee (Hanes, Ball Park hotdogs), Oakley (sunglasses), Quaker Oats (Gatorade), Rayovac, CBS Sportsline (Web site), and WorldCom (MCI).

~

Jordan's plethora of endorsement deals sometimes put him in the middle of clashes between corporate titans. One nasty dispute broke out after Jordan signed a deal in 1995 with Oakley Inc., a California-based maker of sunglasses.

Nike had decided to start its own line of eyewear, prompting Oakley to sue in 1997. Nike returned fire a month later, suing Oakley for its print ad showing Jordan wearing not only sunglasses but an Oakley Drive F beret. Nike, which had a contract with Jordan going back to 1984, contended that Jordan was obligated to wear only Nike clothing in all ads—even a nonathletic beret.

Shortly after the Nike lawsuit was filed, Oakley announced it would manufacture athletic footwear, raising another potential conflict of interest for Jordan, who sat on the Oakley board of directors. Oakley decided to create a separate board—without Jordan on it—for its footwear division.

The dispute had a personal side, too. Nike's Phil Knight and Oakley's Jim Jannard were former friends who had drifted apart after Knight rejected Jannard's proposal that the companies invest together in a line of domestically manufactured athletic shoes. It was left to Jordan to navigate these roiling corporate waters. He told *Sporting News*:

> *"My obligation is to Nike because it was my first corporation. I have an interest in Oakley because of endorsement opportunities and opportunity to create a stylish product. When it starts getting into a gray area I step back. I try not to be put in a predicament to choose."*[29]

~

According to Jordan's mother, her son has always tried to be fair to the companies that pay him for his endorsements. Deloris Jordan was approached to do a commercial for an orange juice company. At the time, Michael was endorsing for Coca-Cola. "You can't do that!" Jordan told his mother. "Coca-Cola owns Minute Maid. If you make that commercial, you'll be competing with Coca-Cola."

She declined the offer, saying that she "appreciated the fact that he'd learned that loyalty, like integrity, is worth more than money."[30]

LOYALTY WORKS BOTH WAYS

After Jordan's second retirement from basketball, the companies he endorsed stuck by him, though Nike planned to change its approach: "We are looking at marketing more Michael the person," said Larry Miller, president of Nike's Jordan Division. "Things like hard work and dedication, excellence, and being prepared. It's not focusing on whether he can score 40 points; it's the characteristics that made Michael able to score 40 points."[31]

Susan D. Wellington, president of the Quaker Oats Company U.S. Gatorade division, told *Business Week*, "Michael has a work ethic and competitiveness that transcend the court. Right now, I'd like to meet the idiot who stops using him."[32]

~

Wall Street investors, however, seemed more concerned about Michael's continuing impact. After all, on October 6, 1993, the day Michael Jordan announced he was retiring from the NBA the first time, the Dow Jones Index was up, except for companies with products endorsed by Jordan. Nike, McDonald's, Sara Lee, Quaker Oats, and General Mills all closed down on the New York Stock Exchange that day.[33]

THE $10 BILLION JORDAN EFFECT

In 1998, *Fortune* magazine systematically took stock of the economic glow Jordan cast over not only the Chicago Bulls but the multitude of businesses he prompted—from sports items to cologne to dessert cakes. Stephen Greyser, professor of marketing at Harvard Business School, told *Fortune*, "His contribution has been a big lift for everybody. He was like the rising tide raising all boats."[34]

One obvious beneficiary was Bulls majority owner

Jerry Reinsdorf, who bought 56 percent of the team for $9.6 million the year after Jordan signed his first contract. The Bulls' estimated worth in 1998 was more than $200 million.

Applying a formula developed by economists Jerry A. Hausman of MIT and Gregory K. Leonard of Cambridge Economics, the magazine calculated that Jordan's impact on NBA attendance—both at home and on the road—increased revenues by $165.5 million during 13 seasons in the NBA.

The sale of NBA merchandise skyrocketed during the Jordan years, from $44 million the year before he joined the league to $1.56 billion in 1990–91 and up to $3.1 billion during the 1995–96 basketball season. According to the Hausman-Leonard formula, Jordan was responsible for $3.1 billion of the gross retail sales in the years he played basketball.

David Falk, Jordan's agent, sold his F.A.M.E. (Falk Associates Management Enterprises) agency to SFX Entertainment for $100 million in cash and incentives. *Fortune* magazine attributed about half the purchase price to F.A.M.E.'s star client, Michael Jordan.

The magazine further estimated the Jordan Effect on television revenues to be at about $366 million.

Other areas that benefited from Jordan's popularity included:

- $5.2 billion for Nike, manufacturer of Air Jordans. The total included $2.6 billion in gross sales of all Jordan products. The remainder was attributed to the impact of Jordan's image on Nike, with its effect on the sales of all the company's products.

- An estimated $408 million increase in corporate revenues as a result of other Jordan endorsements. *Fortune* based this figure on the assumption that companies that hired Jordan expected to gain more than the $240 million they collectively paid him for endorsements between 1990 and 1998.

- $80 million generated by the sale of 4 million of Jordan's sports videos, including the best-selling "Michael Jordan: Come Fly with Me."

- An estimated $17 million from sales of four Michael Jordan books—*Rare Air*, *The Jordan Rules*, *Hang Time*, and *I Can't Accept Not Trying*.
  NOTE: No figures were available for sales of nearly 70 other books on Michael Jordan.

- $155 million in worldwide sales of Michael Jordan cologne, created by Bijan.

- $10 million in annual sales of Michael Jordan men's underwear by Hanes.

- $439 million in revenues from the movie *Space Jam*, far exceeding the $125 million in production and promotion costs, with box office revenues of $230 million and $209 million in video sales.

Furthermore, *Fortune* pointed out that its figures were conservative, stating it could have easily credited other earnings to Jordan. "But isn't that the point? The Jordan effect has been humongous but ultimately immeasurable."[35]

~

Jordan says he is selective in choosing his corporate connections.

"We didn't just pick up every deal we could. We tried to be selective because we wanted to project a certain image, a positive outlook."[36]

But he expressed amazement at how well that strategy ultimately worked.

"I never really envisioned myself having any kind of major impact on people. I never really thought I could persuade them to pursue something I was involved with or buy a product just because I talked about it. Even now, when I see kids wearing my shoes, it's kind of wild. Sometimes I still feel shocked. It's fun, but it's also a lot of responsibility, and I don't take that lightly."[37]

~

Jordan responded to the possibility that his departure from the NBA might put a dent in the economy by saying:

> "Sure, the economy may take a different turn, but I would advise you to invest wisely."[38]

JORDAN, THE ENTREPRENEUR

Jordan's passion for golf meant he had a special interest in launching the Michael Jordan Golf Company, a venture in which he reportedly invested $1 million of his own money.

It was one of the few Jordan-related businesses that, ultimately, did not do well financially. After one golf course and three golf apparel stores opened, Jordan's representatives took control of the company from the founding group and sold it to AMF Bowling Inc. In describing the deal, the *Chicago Tribune* pointed out that AMF executives "readily admit they agreed to take on Jordan Golf and its problems as part of the price for getting Jordan as an endorser for its bowling centers."[39]

~

Like other sports celebrities, Michael Jordan ventured into the restaurant business. At the Original Michael Jordan's, his stylish eatery in Chicago, diners can order (among other things) Jordan's own pregame favorite, a 23-ounce New York strip steak and a baked potato, or watch Bulls games on a 20-by-6-foot video wall in MJ's Fast Break Bar.

The downtown Chicago establishment is lavishly decorated with larger-than-life photographs of its namesake, and the gift shop does a brisk business selling MJ T-shirts, caps, mugs, and dozens of other logo items.

In 1995, Jordan's second restaurant opened in New York City's restored Grand Central Terminal and at last report was doing well.

THE ERA OF THE MEGASALARY

By the standards of the 1980s, Jordan's first contract with the Bulls was generous—a seven-year deal potentially worth more than $6 million. The contract was guaranteed for five years and could be extended for two more. Jonathan Kovler, then Bulls vice president, grumbled a bit that the Bulls "paid through the nose," but said that Jordan was such a great player, he was worth the long-term commitment.

In Jordan's rookie season, when his salary amounted to $550,000, ticket sales rose from about $2 million to $3.8 million, and average home game attendance increased 87 percent over the previous season. The Bulls realized another $190,000 in 1985, when the team with Michael made the playoffs for the first time since 1981.

Jordan would later say the team got a bargain, but as an easygoing 21-year-old, he was pleased:

"My attorneys saw some problems with the contract, but I didn't. I'm happy the negotiations are over, and

anxious to start fitting in with the Bulls. It won't be the Michael Jordan show. I'll just be part of the team."[40]

~

Another indication that money was not Jordan's only career motive was the "love-of-the-game" clause he insisted be included in his contract with the Bulls.

When Jordan entered the professional ranks, the NBA was attempting to reduce the risk of injury to its players. The league's Uniform Players Contract required players to get permission before playing basketball in the off-season. But Jordan would have none of that. The terms of his contract specifically allowed him to play pickup basketball anytime and anywhere he wanted during the off-season.

"I would never offer that to another player," said Bulls general manager Jerry Krause, after discovering the provision.[41]

~

Jordan's earnings soared along with his career. *Forbes* magazine reported that, in addition to his $33 million Chicago Bulls salary for the 1997–98 season, his yearly take for endorsements was $47 million. The magazine estimated that Jordan's total income from his salary and endorsements between 1990 and the end of 1997 exceeded $300 million.[42]

Jordan emphasized that the dollar figures bandied about regarding his earnings were only guesses. He told ABC's *Primetime Live* that he doesn't know how much he makes.

> *"Those are estimates. If I don't know, you think they know?"[43]*

⁓

> *"I play the game because I love it. I just happen to get paid."[44]*

⁓

In September 1988, Jordan signed a new eight-year contract with the Bulls worth $25 million. Three months later, Jordan asked Bulls general manager Jerry Krause if Krause could hire other ball players to help improve the quality of the team. He was told that his salary increase made it impossible because it caused the Bulls to bump up against the NBA's salary cap. Jordan said:

> *"All I know is that my money is hard-earned, and maybe that isn't the case all around. I hate to be singled out as the reason we can't get any more players. It isn't right."[45]*

⁓

Jordan portrayed Bulls owner Jerry Reinsdorf as a tightfisted man who begrudged paying his star player what he deserved. Jordan negotiated a one-year $33 million salary—a figure he thought reflected his true value to the team—for the 1997–98 season. But Reinsdorf ruined it for him, he said, because he ended the session by telling Jordan he knew he would regret the deal one day.

Noting that for some years he had been underpaid, and that during that time the value of the team had skyrocketed, Jordan said:

"That hit me so deep inside—that sense of greed, of disrespect for me."[46]

~

Asked how he would set salaries for key members of the Bulls team, if money wasn't an object, Jordan joked:

"I would pay Michael Jordan $100 million, give Phil [Jackson] $50 million, give Scottie [Pippen] $75 million and move on."[47]

Then he added:

"Oh, Dennis [Rodman] gets $25 million. He's probably worth more, but my budget is really tight."[48]

~

By his retirement in 1999, Jordan's net worth was estimated at $500 million. His vast wealth inspired Kevin Flatley, director of estate planning at Bank-Boston, to send a message to Jordan on the Business Wire: "Now that he's retired, Michael Jordan faces some of the most important decisions of his life: What are the best ways for Michael to protect his estimated $500 million estate?"[49]

Flatley warned that without proper planning, Jordan's family could lose up to 70 percent of his estate to taxes when he dies.

JORDAN, THE LABOR ACTIVIST

Michael Jordan took a strong stand for players by refusing to participate in spring training games as the baseball strike dragged on into early 1995. Instead, he walked away from baseball and went back to basketball.

"I didn't want any part of crossing a picket line."[50]

~

Sadly, when Jordan returned to basketball, labor problems surfaced in that sport, too. In the player–owner NBA dispute of 1995, Jordan, along with Patrick Ewing and some other top players, assumed a prominent role in negotiating for more favorable terms for players.

Jordan and his colleagues objected to the proposal the players' union brought back to its members, describing it as too favorable to NBA management and owners and not good enough to the players.

Particularly galling to the players were the limits the proposal put on exceptions to the salary caps, which the group believed would restrict free agents' movement around the league. The tentative agreement also cut annual salary increases from 30 percent to 20 percent.[51]

Player dissidents made a move to decertify the union.

After the National Labor Relations Board ordered a decertification election, Jordan said:

> *"We're not trying to make sure the league starves or doesn't become successful. If the league is not successful, we can't be successful and we endanger our own position. But we know the league is very successful. We just want an equal opportunity to make our value."*[52]

~

The decertification effort failed after the NBA commissioner hinted that doing so might force a cancellation of the pending 1995–96 season. Of the 361 eligible players who voted, 63 percent favored keeping the union, which cleared the path for the collective bargaining agreement approved by the union and the NBA.[53]

Even so, the group was able to improve on the original contract proposal.

"There's no doubt in my mind that the decertification movement got us a better deal," said Charles Smith, the union's executive vice president. "There's no doubt about it. The only thing that was bad about it was that the union took a hit."[54]

~

When team owners threatened a lockout that would have canceled the 1995–96 season, Jordan, among others, filed an affidavit in the U.S. District Court in Minneapolis supporting an antitrust suit against the league. Jordan argued that a lockout would cut short his basketball career and deprive him of improving his skills to their prebaseball level.

"I will be losing a significant portion of my relatively short and finite NBA career which I will never be able to regain. The greatest harm caused by the cancellation of the 1995–96 NBA season as a result of the 'lockout' will be the loss of NBA basketball for. . . fans, and all of the cities, concession workers, broadcasting employees, and others who depend on the game for their livelihood."[55]

~

After leading his team to win their sixth, and his final, NBA championship in June 1998, Michael Jordan sided with the players during another salary dispute, which this time did lead to a six-month NBA lockout. The dispute came to a head when the National Basketball Association decided to exercise its right to reopen its six-year collective bargaining agreement. Team owners wanted stricter caps on players' salaries. The players resisted.

The NBA lockout began in June, causing the loss of the first part of the season and dragging on until January 6, 1999, just before the NBA's deadline for canceling the entire 1998–99 NBA schedule.

During the lockout, Jordan participated in contract negotiations while refusing to answer questions as to whether he intended to play when the games resumed.

At a Las Vegas meeting of the National Basketball Players Union in October 1998, Jordan said he had not made a decision whether he would play another season:

"But that doesn't mean I shouldn't be a part of the union. I owe an obligation to the young players and the players who came before me."[56]

~

The day Jordan retired in 1999, Scottie Pippen told ABC's *Good Morning America* that he did not think Jordan's departure was due to the six-month NBA lockout, which had ended the previous week. "I think Michael tried to do as much as he can, going through the negotiation," Pippen said. "And he felt at one point that it was probably time for him to take a step back, because a lot was being made of him in saying that, you know, being a client of David Falk [Jordan's agent] that they were in trying to overpower the owners with clients [players].

"So I think Michael just wanted to sort of step away and really show that, hey, I'm out of this, I'm stepping away from the game and pretty much I've done all I can and I've spoken, given you guys my opinion on what I feel the union should do."[57]

~

During his retirement press conference, Michael Jordan said that indeed he delayed the announcement until the lockout ended.

"In the middle of that process with the lockout, I wanted to support the players. I wanted to be there and voice some of the opinions of some of the players and give my input because I felt that as an obligation to the players of tomorrow, just as the players before me stood up and supported the collective bargaining agreement for me to utilize in my negotiations. I felt obligated to do the same."[58]

When the lockout was over, Jordan said, he gave notice to the Bulls so the team could use the $21 million from his canceled contract to help rebuild the team."[59]

GIVING SOMETHING BACK

Jordan created a nonprofit organization, the Michael Jordan Foundation, to help support charitable programs. After his father's death, the foundation was closed. Attention was shifted to the James Jordan Boys and Girls Club, which was built with the help of a $4 million contribution from the Chicago Bulls and $2 million from Jordan to be paid over four years.

∽

In late 1994, Jordan announced he was extending his philanthropic work to focus on the Carolinas.

"This is home. We wanted to extend our hands further into other communities in the nation. Where

would be better to start than North Carolina and South Carolina?"[60]

As part of the same effort, Jordan endowed the Institute for Families at the University of North Carolina at Chapel Hill.

～

On January 28, 1999, just days after retiring from basketball, Michael Jordan launched the $5 million Jordan Fundamentals program to help schools in poor neighborhoods. On behalf of the Jordan Brand, Nike will make a $1 million donation to the program each of the next five years.

In its first year the program will make 400 awards of $2,500 to teachers proposing creative projects. Jordan said:

"We wanted to focus on giving kids an opportunity to excel and achieve their dreams."[61]

～

In response to a request by Howard Buffett, son of investment superstar Warren Buffett, Jordan once participated in two days of fund-raising in Omaha, Nebraska. A county commissioner at the time, Howard flew Jordan to town on a Berkshire Hathaway corporate jet and presented him with a long list of activities. Jordan objected, then winked. He completed the arduous schedule, including a celebrity basketball game in which Jordan ejected Buffett from the game for not wearing Nike shoes.

Before leaving Omaha, Jordan told Buffett, "Howie, I want you to remember one thing. You really owe me one." Howard Buffett was quick to agree, saying that Jordan did more for Omaha in two days than most people could do in two years.[62]

AS FAMOUS AS GOD?

A 1997 *Wall Street Journal* NBC news poll placed Michael Jordan as the third best-liked man in the United States, known by 95 percent of all Americans. According to the poll, the most popular person was retired Army General Colin Powell, followed closely by professional golfer Tiger Woods. Jordan and Powell are African-American and one of Woods' parents is African-American.

The poll further indicated that Jordan and Woods were better liked by white religious fundamentalists than former speaker of the House of Representatives, Republican Newt Gingrich, who was viewed negatively by 41 percent of the respondents and favorably by only 35 percent. By comparison, Jordan received a 65 percent positive and 5 percent negative response, and Woods had a 75 percent positive rating, and only 3 percent negative.[1] In each case, some people had no opinion.

Jordan credits his upbringing and his sense of being "just a normal guy" for helping him cope with living in the limelight, particularly in his early NBA years.

> *"You know you're no different than the next person. You're just lucky or whatever. So you start kind of trying to keep your feet on the ground and do it in a very normal way so that it doesn't appear that you have an attitude or cockiness about you."[2]*

JORDAN, THE RELIGIOUS ICON

Following the 1997 McDonald's championship basketball tournament in Paris, Jordan could not walk the streets of the French capital without being mobbed. The lead paragraph of a story in the Paris daily *France Soir* read, "Michael Jordan is in Paris. That's better than the Pope. It's God in person."[3]

~

Michael Jordan scored a record 63 points in a playoff game against the Boston Celtics on April 20, 1986. Though the Bulls lost in double overtime, 135–131, afterward, Celtics forward Larry "Legend" Bird (today, the coach of the Indiana Pacers) signaled the dawn of the Jordan era: "I think he's God disguised as Michael Jordan. He is the most awesome player in the NBA. Today in Boston Garden, on national TV, in the playoffs, he put on one of the greatest shows of all time. I couldn't believe someone could do that against the Boston Celtics."[4]

~

Michael Jordan can't be replaced, said New Jersey Nets player Jayson Williams: "He's Jesus in tennis shoes."[5]

SUPERMAN

Anita DeFrantz, president of the Amateur Athletic Federation of Los Angeles, in 1995 described the Jordan aura by saying that, "Mr. Jordan is from another planet; he is not a mere mortal. He is so far removed from day-to-day life . . . Even the 'bad stuff' he does is so removed from the commonplace citizen it doesn't relate to me."[6]

~

In 1988, Chuck Daly, then coach of the Detroit Pistons, commented: "He's Superman. I don't know how he does it, where he gets that energy, his intelligence, his instinct for the game."[7]

~

Jordan never let irrational hero worship obscure the fact that he is just another human being. When at the 1992 summer Olympic Games in Barcelona, a foreign journalist asked him, "Are you of this Earth?" Jordan replied, "Well, I come from Chicago."[8]

~

"People can fly. Some fly higher than others, that's all."[9]

THE MYTHICAL HERO

The myth of Michael Jordan has soared far beyond the sports world. Reviewing the scholarly work, *War Music*, writer Michael O'Leary strayed away from author Christopher Logue's translation of the *Iliad* to find in Jordan a modern-day parallel to the Greek mythical hero Achilles. O'Leary cited Jordan's remarkable will when he rose from his sickbed in Salt Lake City to lead his team to a crucial victory in Game 5 of the 1997 NBA championship series against the Utah Jazz. In Jordan's determination to stay in the game, Logue found a contemporary metaphor for the *meinin*, or wrath of Achilles, as expressed in the *Iliad*:

"What emerged that night was both staggering and dreadful," wrote O'Leary. "What won that game was Jordan's will, stripped down to its dark, bare dreadful essence. But it wasn't even so much a matter of choice: Jordan's purpose and burden was to win at all costs. And there is something both horrifying and awe-inspiring about that urge, especially when laid so bare as on that night. Jordan's will is the only thing in this day and age that approaches the scope of the unknowable *meinin* of Achilles."[10]

Jordan said he has found his own heroes on familiar territory—at home.

"My heroes were my parents. I can't see having anyone else as my heroes. Because of the situation I'm in, I've seen a lot of what people expect in heroes. People expect their heroes to be flawless, never to make mistakes, to be happy all the time. And no one can do that. No one never makes mistakes, and no one always does everything right, and I can tell you for sure that no one is happy all the time."[11]

Through the years, other accomplished athletes took their turn at paying homage to Jordan's athleticism. In a 1997 interview in *Esquire* magazine, star hockey player Wayne Gretzky dismissed comparisons of himself to Michael Jordan: "I hear people talk about me sometimes in the same breath as Michael, as though I'm the Michael of hockey. And I just want to laugh. No one belongs in the same breath as Michael. That's not just modesty. That's just fact."[12]

SOMEONE WHO DOESN'T IDOLIZE MJ?

After *Time* magazine published a cover story on Jordan after the Chicago Bulls' sixth NBA championship, both fans and critics responded strongly. Here is one of the letters published in the magazine:

"I'll be damned if I'm going to idolize someone who gets paid millions of dollars just because he's got a good jump shot. You made Jordan out to be the equivalent of Mahatma Gandhi, when all he has done is play a game well." —Sam Jones, age 17, Tampa, Florida

~

Chicago sportswriter Sam Smith said it upset Jordan when Smith wrote the book *The Jordan Rules*, which was critical of the superstar: "I wrote he was a trash talker and that he insults his teammates and was a hard guy to get along with," Smith told *Editor & Publisher* magazine. "He wasn't used to being criticized because he had suck-ups all around him."[13]

Smith wrote a second book about Jordan, in which he said many fans cherish a favorite memory of Michael Jordan on the court: "But I most recall this: a Thursday afternoon in October 1991, when Jordan walked out of a Bulls practice, stopped, shot me a hard look in the eye, and said, 'You're a fucking asshole,'" wrote Smith.[14]

FAME: THE JOB THAT NEVER ENDS

In September 1994, when General Mills sponsored a reunion of its box-cover athletes, Michael Jordan stole the show. Bob Richards, who won an Olympic gold medal for pole vaulting, recalled that "When Michael came in, the press and the guests politely walked by all the rest of us. There was this aura in the room, Michael's aura, and everyone was drawn to it. The rest of us were nonexistent."[15]

~

Fame, says Jordan, comes with a psychological burden:

> *"No matter how hard I try, I'm never going to be the perfect person. The one time I tell somebody that I'm tired and that I don't want to sign another autograph, that person gets a whole different feeling about Michael Jordan. So my job really never ends."*[16]

~

Esquire magazine described a scene at New York's elegant Plaza Hotel on a day that Michael Jordan was there for breakfast. Jordan's presence "made the lobby of the hotel busier than it was for *Home Alone 2*. Jordan appears suddenly in the doorway, helped by security. He sports an elegant topcoat and a black beret, and smiles at the kids, almost oblivious to the Beatles-in-'64 stir he has created.

"Before he gets to the bus, he sees a face he knows and waves. 'You ever get tired of this?' Michael Jordan is asked. 'You get used to it,' he says and then walks up the steps and goes and takes his seat at the back of the bus."[17]

~

After Jordan filmed a segment for *60 Minutes*, its producer Bill Brown asked himself whether he could find fault with the basketball superstar. "Jordan is absolutely a young man totally at ease with destiny. He is comfortable with his role as a superstar. He is also very alert to the possibilities of the pressures on him. He is totally comfortable with his role in life. Even if his celebrity went away, he would be comfortable with himself."[18]

~

To be sure, Jordan seems to love the glitzy part of fame, the fancy cars, designer clothes, and the Cuban cigars.

He made the cover of *GQ* in 1989 and again in 1996, sharing Man of the Year honors with movie star Mel Gibson and comedian Jerry Seinfeld. Along with a profile, *GQ* featured a close-up full-page photo of the grinning athlete, a gold ring in his ear and a cigar clenched between his teeth.

~

Nevertheless, Jordan said he has never found comfort in the spotlight:

"Your moods start to change. People start taking advantage of your niceness. And you want more time for yourself."[19]

~

Jordan's longtime personal assistant and driver George Koehler says he feels sorry for Michael.

"People tell me they want to be rich and famous. I tell 'em, 'Just be rich.' Michael's had 14 years of this nonsense. I wouldn't blame him for wanting to retire."[20]

SOMEONE WHO NEVER HEARD OF MJ?

When Ted Koppel of ABC News *Nightline* traveled to rural Honduras in November 1998 to interview victims of Hurricane Mitch, he found a woman in the village of Guacamaya clad in a Chicago Bulls championship T-shirt. Through a translator, the woman told Koppel that the shirt had been donated and that she had never heard of Michael Jordan. Duly impressed, Koppel ended the *Nightline* segment solemnly:

"A lot in life, sometimes everything, depends on your perspective. Last week back in the United States, for example, we were all obsessed with Newt Gingrich, Jesse 'The Body' Ventura and John Glenn's magnificent journey into space. This week, we find ourselves in a small village in Honduras where they haven't even heard of Michael Jordan."[21]

THE AUTOGRAPH SEEKERS

In 1998, Michael Jordan played golf at The Farms, an upscale, private course in Rancho Santa Fe, California, where he has a membership. Jordan was surrounded and besieged for autographs. The club management promptly sent a crossly worded memo to its wealthy and well-known members, reminding them that many people join the club for privacy, and therefore they should respect the privacy of others. Even the rich and famous seem dazzled by Jordan's presence.

∽

After the original U.S. Olympic Dream Team swept the Barcelona games, Jordan said that at one time he could visit Paris without being mobbed for autographs, but even that refuge was now gone:

> *"It's just hard for me to go anywhere now unnoticed—in the sense of getting out in the public and trying to enjoy myself without people bothering me. This was the last area that I could go to where no one really knew who I was to some degree. And now it's been exposed."*[22]

∽

On one occasion, Jordan was driving away from the Bulls' practice facility in his white Porsche 911 turbo when two cars cut him off, forcing him to stop. Out of one car jumped two autograph seekers. Out of the other jumped a man waving a blue sweatsuit with an Air Jordan logo on it and demanding to talk to Jordan about a potential deal. "Believe it or not," said Jordan, "that wasn't all that unusual."[23]

Chicago Tribune columnist Bob Greene wrote about one incident when crowds gathered at a Chicago White Sox baseball practice to get autographs from Jordan. When Jordan stopped to oblige, adults in the back rows began pushing so hard that a small child in the front was smashed against the metal meshing of the waist-high fence. The parents, excited to see Jordan, failed to see what was happening. But Jordan did. "Stop it," Jordan yelled to the crowd. "There's kids up here." Then he reached down and rescued the sobbing, gasping boy.[24]

~

Despite the annoyance, Jordan was generous with autographs.

"I'm a soft-hearted person. Rarely do I say no. I'll sign autographs all day. Patrick Ewing and others, they'll say no. Myself, I can't do that."[25]

~

But Jordan says that as a kid, he never asked for autographs, and he does not relate personally to the demand for his signature. He has tried to avoid public autograph sessions since an incident when he was nearly stampeded in Houston.

"The autograph stuff drives me crazy. People are dangerous."[26]

~

JORDAN MEMORABILIA

In an exhibit case at the Cape Fear Museum in Wilmington, North Carolina, where Michael Jordan grew up, is a pay stub, totaling $119.76, earned by Jordan as a teen-ager. The stub came from a part-time maintenance job he briefly held at H.L. "Whitey" Prevatte's El-Berta Motor Inn and Restaurant.

"That thing has sent me a lot of business," Prevatte said. "I had people from Germany come in here one time asking about him because they saw the stub at the museum."[27]

~

The sale of sports equipment and memorabilia signed by superstars like Michael Jordan is a lucrative business, and merchants ask for and get top dollar. During the 1998 Christmas season, for instance, the Field of Dreams store in San Diego's Horton Plaza offered a number 23 Bulls jersey signed by Michael Jordan for $2,295.

As the value of Jordan items grew, so did the potential for fakery. An increasing number of items allegedly signed by sports heroes turn out to be forged, causing headaches for legitimate vendors and law enforcement.

One company has made a business of authenticating Jordan's signature. Upper Deck Authenticated, the official marketer for Michael Jordan memorabilia, set up a five-step process to ensure that customers would know they are buying the real thing. Under a contract, Jordan (among other sports superstars), signs sports memorabilia in front of Upper Deck representatives at least once a month. Jordan reassures customers buying his signed items in an Upper Deck promotional video, "You'll get a letter of authenticity with that, which basically states, hey, he signed it. We saw him sign it and you know it's the real thing."[28]

~

Yahoo! held an Internet auction for Michael Jordan trading cards. The action was particularly heavy the day after Jordan's second retirement announcement.

On January 14, 1999, with one day of bidding left, a 1995–96 Skybox Emotion Michael Jordan Card No. 100 drew 13 bids, the highest at $69. The card showed Jordan with number 45 on his jersey, which he wore only briefly before going back to number 23.

At the other end of the price scale, a 1997–98 Michael Jordan number 23 Z-Force card drew six bids, with the highest only at $3.[29]

~

At an auction in June 1997, a Japanese businessman paid $22,000 for a pair of 1986 Air Jordan basketball shoes that had been worn by Jordan.[30]

~

While his presence has brought pleasure to millions of his fans, there is an ominous side to Jordan's fame. One of the most troubling is the exaggerated value attached to his memorabilia and Jordan-endorsed sportswear. In 1998, a fan climbed into the rafters of the University of North Carolina Smith Center and stole the retired number 23 jersey Michael Jordan wore during his college basketball years. It had been on display along with the retired jerseys of five other outstanding North Carolina players.[31]

His fans have sometimes been driven to steal, even to kill, to get hold of it. When shown a news account of a Maryland boy robbed and killed for his new Air Jordans, Michael said: "I can't believe it. Choked to death by his friend . . ." After mulling over the episode of sneaker violence, he added:

"I thought I'd be helping out others and everything would be positive. I thought people would try to emulate the good things I do, they'd try to achieve, to be better. Nothing bad. I never thought because of my endorsement of a shoe, or any product, that people would harm each other. Everyone likes to be admired, but when it comes down to kids actually killing each other, you have to reevaluate things."[32]

THE OTHER MICHAEL JORDANS

While a lot of his fans—especially the younger ones—want to be like Mike, one of his fellow North

Carolinians actually is like Mike. Lee Kealon bears an uncanny resemblance to the superstar and is often mistaken for him.

Like Michael Jordan, Kealon is 6-feet 6-inches, wears size 14 shoes, and shaves his head. Both were born in Brooklyn and grew up in Wilmington, North Carolina, where Kealon still lives. Both love to play golf. And although one clearly is the world's best basketball's player, Kealon likes to play, too. He's been known to don a number 23 jersey and play at the same park Michael Jordan frequented when he was a boy.

Kealon described his one meeting with Michael Jordan at the 1995 opening of the Jordan exhibit at the Cape Fear Museum. Kealon arrived first and found himself surrounded by Jordan fans. The real Michael Jordan slipped in later.

When he was introduced to Jordan, Kealon recalled: "The first thing [Jordan] said to me was, 'Are you the one causing the big commotion outside?'"[33]

~

Another who has to put up with comparisons to the basketball star is a guard on the University of Pennsylvania's basketball team, who just happens to be named Michael Jordan. At the time his parents named him, the "real" Jordan was still an unknown high school kid. The University of Pennsylvania Jordan wears number 23 on his jersey too, the number of his famous counterpart. And his team switched from Reebok shoes to Nike, the star's preferred brand.

The *Wall Street Journal* reported that the lesser-known Jordan has to endure trash talk from opponents, who taunt, "You're not the real Michael Jordan!"

The younger Jordan said he has a sense of humor about playing in the reflected light of the other Michael Jordan. "You have to laugh at some of it," he said. "I find it very amusing."[34]

~

An essay on the perils of cloning in the *New Republic* magazine discussed the reasons why one Michael Jordan should suffice:

"If there were basketball teams fielding Jordans against Jordans, we wouldn't be able to recognize the one, the only, Michael Jordan. It's like suggesting that forty Mozarts are better than one. There would be no Mozart if there were forty Mozarts. We know the singularity of the one, the extraordinary genius—a Jordan, a Mozart—because they stand apart from and above the rest. Absent that irreducible singularity, their gifts and glorious accomplishments would mean nothing. They would be the norm, commonplace: another dunk, another concerto."[35]

~

Jordan is a self-described people person, but after his first several years in the NBA, the constant crush of adoring fans began to weigh on him.

"People say they wish they were Michael Jordan. Okay, do it for a year. Do it for two years. Do it for five years. When you get past the fun part, then go do the part where you get into cities at 3:00 A.M. and you have 15 people waiting for autographs when you're as tired as hell."[36]

THE MAN
BEHIND THE IDOL

Michael Jordan wowed fans with nearly superhuman feats on the court. But who is he really? An ordinary person, blessed with extraordinary talent and a ferocious will to win. He has likes and dislikes, he jokes, smokes cigars, and plays cards with his friends.

He sometimes seems so thunderstruck by his success that he talks about Michael Jordan, the player, in the third person. He once said that basketball is:

> *"[T]he link between the real Michael Jordan and the public Michael Jordan. Take away basketball, and it's hard to get to the real Michael Jordan."*[1]

~

Jordan explains that he held onto his humanity and connected well with the public because he never tried to be something he wasn't.

> *"The word 'image,' well, that's something you put on. My image is me. For better or worse."*[2]

~

Because his comments are so widely reported, Jordan has learned to keep some thoughts to himself. In 1995, after reporters had questioned him on his reactions to the Oklahoma City terrorist bombing, Jordan asserted his right to keep his views out of the limelight.

"I have controversial thoughts, but the media might not understand and take it the wrong way if I say them."[3]

~

Jordan is seen as a complex person, even by those near to him. "I think I analyze him [Jordan] pretty good," said Bulls Assistant Coach Tex Winter, "but he's a mystery man in a lot of ways, and I think he always will be, maybe even to himself."[4]

BASKETBALL'S BLITHE SPIRIT

Michael Jordan was intense on court, but he also had a playful, fun-loving side, as NBA player Muggsy Bogues discovered. Bogues—at 5-feet 3-inches the shortest player in the league—and the 6-foot 6-inch Jordan came out of a locker room together for the 1991 All-Star Stay in School JAM. Putting his hand on Bogues's head, Jordan asked:

"Listen, did anyone lose their child?"[5]

Four years later, Bogues got his revenge at another charitable basketball event held the summer after Jordan quit baseball to renew his pro basketball career.

At the Unlimited Basketball Camp in Greensboro, North Carolina, the nimble Bogues gave Jordan fits. When Jordan drove in for one of his slam-dunks, Bogues surprised him by batting the ball out of bounds. Jordan laughed:

"No, no, Bogues, you can't do that to me. I'm back!"[6]

~

Los Angeles Times sportswriter J.A. Adande spotted Michael Jordan near the locker rooms at Chicago Stadium before a crucial 1993 playoff game between the Bulls and the New York Knicks. The Bulls needed to win in order to even the series at 2–2 as they moved toward their third straight NBA championship.

Jordan was entertaining a small group of security people and cheerleaders, strutting around, his head bobbing like a chicken. Every few steps, he would stop, hold up three fingers and, in a high falsetto, squeak, "Three-peat." Wrote Adande, "The most pressure-packed night of the season, and this was what the world's greatest player was doing to prepare for the game."[7]

~

Although Jordan's wit often was aimed at others, he poked fun at himself, too. In 1991, he appeared on NBC's *Saturday Night Live*, making light of his wholesome commercial image. In an SNL spoof, Jordan pretended to endorse a feminine hygiene product called Feminine Secret and his own line of adult videos.[8]

OR NOT SO BLITHE

Michael Jordan could be impatient with less-gifted players, especially if he thought they weren't trying hard enough. His competitive drive occasionally caused him to ridicule lesser mortals or lose his temper, though not severely and not often.

When an angry (then) Golden State Warriors player, Latrell Sprewell, scandalized the sports world by attacking his coach, P.J. Carlesimo, Jordan was dumbfounded, noting that Carlesimo "yells and curses, but you have to be immune to that."

"I can't imagine ever getting that mad at a coach, to the point where you want to physically assault him."[9]

~

Sportswriter Sam Smith wrote that Jordan had a cutting wit, frequently aimed at a teammate. He recalled an incident on board the team's plane after the Chicago Bulls lost a playoff game to the Detroit Pistons. Jordan walked past teammate Horace Grant, picking up Grant's dinner tray as he went, telling him, "You didn't play well enough to deserve to eat."[10]

~

Jordan made no secret of his unhappiness with Bulls general manager Jerry Krause, who sometimes found himself on the receiving end of Jordan's pointed humor. *Sport* magazine reported that after a 1997 playoff game, Jordan yelled jibes from the back of the team bus at Krause, who was sitting at the front. "Hey, Jerry Krause, let's go fish. It's B.Y.O.P. Bring Your Own Pole. Don't worry. If we don't catch anything, you can just eat the bait yourself."

Jordan also reportedly yelled, "Hey, Jerry Krause, this bus went faster yesterday without your fat ass on it!"

Krause rarely responded, although he sometimes would mutter, "The mouth from North Carolina is at it again."[11]

~

Chicago Tribune sports columnist Skip Bayless described the basketball icon as part Michael and part Jordan: "The Michael Jordan I choose to remember is the one so many chose not to see. I choose to remember the man's man who was more Jordan than Michael, the cigar-smoking, earring-wearing, trash-talking warrior, the most psychologically intimidating bully that basketball has ever known, the sly, quick-fisted street-ball king, the all-time selfish shooter who played defense as relentlessly as offense, the seething competitor who interpreted the most innocent comments from rivals as personal attacks, the supremely talented overachiever who practiced at least as furiously as he played—the best and baddest ever."[12]

~

When asked about accusations that he was confrontational, Jordan told *Newsweek*:

"I'm a tough competitor, no doubt about that, but I wouldn't say I am confrontational at all. You have to really get me steamed for a confrontation, and that hasn't happened yet. I think that comes from the slow pace of growing up in the South. My grandparents used to always say: 'Think before you act, and be in control at all times.' I always remembered that."[13]

TAKE OFF YOUR SHOES IN THE HOUSE

Jordan's college roommate Buzz Peterson recalled that once, after he had been called away to visit a sick aunt, he returned to find his and Jordan's apartment in immaculate condition, "the whole room cleaned up, my closet fixed, my bed made, and my shoes and sweaters in the right place. That's the kind of person he is."[14]

∿

When he moved to Chicago to join the Bulls, Jordan kept his suburban bachelor pad clean and orderly, which caught the attention of visitors.

A *Sports Illustrated* reporter, invited in along with three other guests on a snowy winter day in 1989, recounted how Jordan ordered all of them to take off their shoes before stepping on his beige rug. Michael's longtime friend, Adolph Shiver, objected. "Uh-uh, take them off," Jordan insisted.[15]

MARRIAGE AND FAMILY

A friend introduced Michael Jordan to Juanita Vanoy, an executive secretary with the American Bar Association, at a restaurant following a Chicago Bulls game in his rookie year. He said she was not overwhelmed at meeting a professional basketball player. Jordan told *Playboy* magazine:

> *"Girls who chase you aren't the ones you're interested in."*[16]

～

Michael describes his wife as "very caring," intelligent, and "a very friendly, outgoing person." She said she was won over by his "big heart," his concern for the less fortunate, and his close family ties.

"He's affectionate and romantic," Juanita said. "We often have candlelight dinners. He likes champagne, and he sends me flowers all the time."[17]

～

Michael and Juanita were married at the Little White Chapel on the Las Vegas Strip in September 1989. Juanita was 30 at the time and the mother of Michael's 10-month-old son, Jeffrey. Michael was 26. The ceremony, held at 3:30 A.M., was relaxed. The bride and groom both wore jeans. He gave her a five-karat marquise diamond ring.

The superstar believes that a stable marital relationship and children gave him an important focus away from basketball. Two years after their marriage, and by then the father of two, Jordan told *Ebony* magazine:

> *"As a father, I just want to be there for my kids. To help them learn, to help them enjoy life and yet, give them discipline, guidance."*[18]

～

The Jordans had their second son, Marcus James Jordan, in December 1990, and their daughter, Jasmine, in December 1992.

～

The Jordans live in Highland Park, near Chicago. Their 22,000-square-foot home sits on seven acres of land; it has an indoor basketball court, indoor-outdoor pool, a hot tub, and a sauna. Juanita generally lives quietly and keeps a low profile. Michael said:

> *"She's not the partying type, and neither am I."*[19]

～

The Jordans, however, have explained what they like about each other. Michael said:

> *"She always was very independent. She knew how to work and provide for herself, which is what I loved."*[20]

Juanita recalled she was apprehensive about dating an athlete four years her junior. "He proved his maturity to me, and he has this big heart," she said.[21]

Michael said he has trouble turning down requests from family, friends, and even strangers. His wife helps on that score. "I have no problem saying no," Juanita said. "If someone doesn't step up and say no, there would be no time for his family. Everyone wants a piece of Michael. When people see him, they feel it's their only chance to get an autograph, touch him, shake his hand. And he just can't say no.

"I know it makes me look like a bitch, but I can't worry about it because I'm protecting what we have. If that is what I have to be, then I will be a bitch. Call me what you like."[22]

A CRUEL HOAX

When playing, Jordan was so concerned about his family's well-being that he could not concentrate on a basketball game until he was sure family members who planned to attend were in their seats.

His mother recalled a time when rain snarled traffic, causing the Jordans to be late for their son's college game at the University of North Carolina. To their surprise, the game was delayed until they arrived.

Deloris Jordan said a UNC assistant coach greeted them in the lobby, telling them that their son saw their empty seats, and that "Coach [Dean] Smith didn't want to start the game with Michael so worried, so we decided to delay the tip-off as long as we could."[23]

The Jordans took their seats, Michael smiled up at them, and the game began.

～

In December 1997, during a Chicago Bulls game against the Minnesota Timberwolves in Minneapolis, a phone call came into the stadium during halftime. The caller stated that Jordan's mother, Deloris, had been taken to a North Carolina hospital. The voice on the phone identified himself as Larry, the name of Jordan's brother.

Though it turned out to be a sick prank, Jordan did not find out until after the game that his mother was fine. Distraught, Jordan returned to the game in the second half but missed 10 of his last 14 shots. The Bulls lost 99–95.

> *"It was tough focusing. The game really didn't have the same meaning, because you really didn't know. There was a lot of unknown questions there. Fortunately it was just a hoax."*[24]

～

Jordan's tight bond with his family was never more obvious than when Jordan retired for the second time. He said that although his mother and brothers and sisters were unable to attend the event in Chicago's United Center:

> *"As you see me, you see them. My father, my mother, and certainly my brothers and sisters, so they are*

159

here through me. They along with myself say thank
you for taking me in and showing the respect and
certainly the gratitude that you have shown me over
the years that I have been here."[25]

ON CHILDREN

Jordan has always had a special affinity for children.
In his first year as a pro, he went out and bought
McDonald's certificates to hand out on Halloween Eve.

To his disappointment, a Bulls game forced him to
be out of town. Michael left a message on his front
door: "Kids: Sorry I missed you for Halloween. If you
still want trick-or-treat, come back in three days."[26]

~

When former Chicago Bulls coach Doug Collins ran a
summer basketball camp at Concordia, a small college
west of Chicago, Michael Jordan thrilled attendees
by showing up to play. One 15-year-old managed to
get around the superstar for a layup attempt, causing
Jordan to tease the boy, who wasn't wearing Michael's
Nike brand, "You got the other guy's shoes on and
everything."

When Jordan took a shot, the kid jammed him.
"Your mom and dad up in the stands?" asked Jordan,
delighting the onlookers and making an instant
celebrity of the youngster.[27]

~

Time permitting, Jordan would visit children's hospitals to cheer up sick and disabled kids. During one such visit in Pittsburgh, he called the youngsters "partners" and got them to laugh. Carrying a basketball net and rim, when he came upon a bedridden child, he pulled the rim close to the bed so that the youngster could put a ball through the basket. "You can't go back to sleep until you make one," he told the child.[28]

~

Daniel Ames, a New Hampshire 13-year-old, wrote this poem, published in *Sports Illustrated for Kids*:

> M.J. was cut from his high school team,
> But the future Bull, he had a dream.
> He'd show them all he is the best,
> and, since then, well, you know the rest.
> He's been the man in the NBA
> From rookie year up through today.
> Come finals time, fans scream and shout
> As Jordan wins, his tongue hanging out.[29]

~

Jordan's popularity extended even to the children of his opponents. In 1997, Utah Jazz guard Jeff Hornacek was nonplussed that his 9-year-old son, Ryan, preferred to wear a Jordan jersey when his Dad's team played the Bulls in the NBA Finals.

But Hornacek said he understood his kids' admiration for basketball's chief luminary. "Who doesn't like

Michael Jordan?" Hornacek said. "They go upstairs on their little tykes' baskets, and they're not pretending they're me dunking the ball. They're pretending they're Michael."[30]

~

Jordan says his own children like to visit beaches and amusement parks, though he doesn't go on the rides with them because they make him "a little sick." Despite his fame, Jordan says his kids have normal lives—most of the time:

> *"The only problems they have are when we are out and people want my autograph. My kids want to spend time with me and not have people interrupt us."[31]*

MJ says his greatest joy is "[J]ust watching my kids. They never have bad days. And if I'm having a bad day, when I see them, it's not a bad day anymore."[32]

KIDS, DON'T STICK YOUR TONGUE OUT

When Jordan retired for the first time in 1993, he joked about his trademark: sticking out his tongue during intense play on-court.

> *"My special contribution was the tongue. You never saw anything like it, and you won't see anything like it again."[33]*

~

Youngsters who wanted to be like Mike began to emulate his habit of sticking out his tongue as he drove to the basket. It was, perhaps, an inherited trait, Jordan said. His father had also let his tongue hang out when he was busily working on one of his home mechanical projects.

"Coach [Dean] Smith wanted me to stop it when I was back at UNC. But it's not a conscious thing. I can't play with it in."[34]

Jordan feared that youngsters might bite off their tongues if they tried to be too much like him. He warned:

"For your tongues' sake, kids, don't do it."[35]

I NEVER SEE YOU FOR YOUR COLOR

Jordan was a teenager when he saw the dramatic television mini-series on black history, *Roots*, and it made him very angry:

"It was a very tough year. I was really rebelling. I considered myself a racist at that time. Basically, I was against all white people."[36]

~

Jordan's family helped him to realize that racial incidents of the past shouldn't hold him back today, that he should work to make a better world. They endowed him with a deep sense of racial equality that has been with him since childhood.

Jordan says his parents helped him get over his racial anger, but it took about a year.

"You have to be able to say 'OK, that happened back then. Now let's take it from here and see what happens.' It would be very easy to hate people for the rest of your life, and some people have done that. You've got to deal with what's happening now and try and make things better."[37]

～

Jordan grew up with David Bridges, a white boy from his hometown; he had a white roommate in college, Buzz Peterson; and formed a lasting friendship with George Koehler, whom he met when Koehler gave him a ride from the airport when Jordan first arrived in Chicago. But he also has many close African-American friends, among them Adolph Shiver and Fred Whitfield, whom he had known since childhood.

"They're all very close to me. I don't believe in race. I believe in friendship."[38]

～

Sociologists have found racial implications in the adulation of an African-American athlete. John Hoberman of the University of Texas, who has studied and written about African-Americans in sports, described the phenomenon this way:

"The reason for the absurd dimensions of the cult of Michael Jordan is directly related to the depth of the racial crisis in the United States. The way we look at Michael Jordan constitutes pseudo-race relations, a way to accept black men into a society extremely concerned about their behavior. The more U.S. society fears black males, the more it invests in a false relationship with a black superstar. It doesn't involve the complexities of dealing with a black colleague, teacher, policeman, or neighbor. It is 'virtual integration.'"[39]

~

Jordan's teammate and friend Charles Barkley seems to agree with Hoberman's assessment: "Michael Jordan, Eddie Murphy, Arsenio Hall, these people are not treated the same as other blacks in society," said Barkley. "You might listen to black music and you might watch black athletes, but that doesn't mean you'll be willing to talk to that black guy who just moved down the street."[40]

~

Essence magazine offered a gentler portrait of Jordan's impact on society, saying he occupies "the enviable, extraordinary, and undoubtedly taxing position of African-American hero—with equal emphasis placed on the African and the American. His achievement comes in an era when unqualified Black male heroism is rare and thus particularly precious. While White-chosen heroes (Christopher Darden, Clarence Thomas), flawed icons (Tupac Shakur, Mike Tyson), and polarizing forces (Marion Barry, Louis Far-rakhan) proliferate, Jordan has universal respect from women and men, Blacks and Whites and children of all ages."[41]

LIKE SPIN-OFFS FROM A HIT TV SITCOM

George Koehler has remained Jordan's driver and personal assistant throughout Jordan's years in basketball and baseball.

Koehler says he feels privileged to "hang out with Michael."

"Fifteen years ago, when I first met Michael here in Chicago, I was the very first person he met in this city. That was when I had a limousine company. He will tell you that I have been taking him for a ride ever since then."[42]

∼

Jordan keeps the welcome mat out for Adolph Shiver and his other North Carolina buddies. His friends have basked in Jordan's reflected glory, and have become minor celebrities because of their friendship with Michael. "They're like spinoffs from a hit TV show," noted *Los Angeles Times* sportswriter J.A. Adande.[43]

∼

One of Jordan's most meaningful friendships is with Gus Lett, a security guard at Chicago Stadium whom

Jordan met when Lett helped Jordan carry his gear when he broke his foot during his second season with the Bulls.

Lett bore a physical resemblance to Jordan's father and, after James Jordan was murdered, Lett became like a second father and personal adviser.

When Lett developed malignant tumors in his brain and chest, Jordan personally saw to it that Lett received the best medical care.

"He means a lot to me. When you look at Gus, the game really doesn't mean as much. Because he is struggling through something that means a little bit more than playing a basketball game. He is certainly a positive influence for me. I enjoy him being around."[44]

~

AND THEN THERE'S GOLF

Basketball was his career, but golf is Michael Jordan's passion. Jordan has been known to play up to 54 holes in a day, traveling to golf courses across the nation and abroad. Jordan has been a dues-paying member of the Wynstone Golf Club in Chicago; Wexford in Hilton Head, South Carolina; The Farms in Rancho Santa Fe, California; and the Governor's Club in Chapel Hill.[45]

"When I'm on the golf course, I'm at peace."[46]

~

Jordan started playing golf the summer after he left the University of North Carolina to join to the NBA. Davis Love III, who also attended North Carolina and was a member of the PGA tour, got Jordan started by lending him his clubs. Love complained that on one occasion Jordan hit the ball hard enough to break his favorite driver. Jordan thought Love was feigning his distress. "It was already cracked. Davis set me up."[47]

~

"Putting is a lot like shooting free throws. It's all concentration and technique. There's a correct way for the ball to come off your club, the same as there's a correct way for it to come off your fingertips."[48]

~

A golf course may not be the place for trash talk, but Joel Hirsch, one of Michael Jordan's golf buddies, described Jordan as a "chatterer," fond of tormenting his opponents on the fairway. Jordan is an intensely competitive golfer (currently a 3 handicap), and Hirsch remembered Jordan's reaction when he missed on the final hole, costing him the game.

"When he missed that putt, it was like he blew a shot at the NBA Finals," Hirsch said. "He was a perfect gentleman, but you can tell when he walked off the green, he was burning inside."[49]

~

"It was a lot of fun," said Michael Jordan of his participation in the Bob Hope Chrysler Classic in La Quinta, California, one week after he officially retired from the NBA in 1999. Jordan played with his long-time friend Charles Barkley.

Jordan's fans created a traffic jam into Bermuda Dunes, site of the golf tournament, where they hoped to get a glimpse of the NBA icon.[50]

MICHAEL JORDAN
IN HOLLYWOOD

STARRING IN THE TOONS

In Michael Jordan's first venture onto the big screen he co-starred with Bugs Bunny in *Space Jam*. When asked if Bugs Bunny showed up for rehearsals for the cartoon/live-action movie, Jordan replied, "No. He always sent his double. It made it a little tougher for me, but that's the big time, man. You can do that when you've been a star for 60 to 70 years."[1]

Jordan's answer was obviously tongue-in-cheek, but when he met with the media in 1996 just before the release of the film, Jordan explained how the person-to-cartoon character conversations were done. He spoke his lines to human actors, who stood in for the animated characters which were computer-generated into the film.

Jordan also said that acting brought out his shyness:

"I was afraid to let some of the emotions go through me. I was confined by my embarrassment. I'd rather it would have been private. Very few people know me. The less people, the more comfortable I felt."[2]

~

Ivan Reitman of Warner Brothers, who produced *Space Jam*, seemed to think MJ had stage presence:

"There's something in Michael Jordan's face that I felt could work on the screen. He's got these great eyes that communicate, and the light inside of them shines as brightly as any movie star's I've ever seen."[3]

~

Even so, Jordan expressed uncertainty over his future in films.

"I don't know if I'm any good. I'm afraid to have high expectations. In basketball, I control far more. There's so much unknown here."[4]

~

Warner Brothers invested $125 million to produce and promote *Space Jam*, possibly contributing to Jordan's jitters. He needn't have worried. The film grossed about $230 million at the box office and racked up more than $209 million in video sales.

~

Because Jordan was also determined to get back in top basketball condition following his late-season return to the NBA the previous spring, during the filming of *Space Jam*, the studio provided him with all the perks a basketball star who had to work out every day could want. Studio execs had a workout gym and a regulation-size basketball court built near the set, where Jordan invited his NBA pals for pickup games when he wasn't filming.

~

It was no surprise that Michael Jordan's first venture on the silver screen was a children's movie. Children comprise a huge percentage of Michael Jordan's fans. The *Sports Illustrated for Kids* Readers' Poll in December 1997 ranked Michael Jordan as the favorite male athlete among more than 7,500 boys and girls who responded to the survey. Among the girls, Jordan topped the list; his pal and teammate Scottie Pippen came in second.

The poll also revealed how Jordan's popularity among young female athletes had impacted the sport in general. In the survey, more girls (43 percent) ranked basketball as their favorite sport to play compared to 28 percent of the boys. A slightly higher number of boys—29 percent—favored football. As to televised sports, 43 percent of the girls said basketball was their favorite. In contrast, 44 percent of the boys listed football as their top choice; 25 percent ranked basketball number 1.[5]

~

As for his future in the movies, Jordan said his roles may be limited:

> *"My wife already said if I wanna do this, 'No nude shots and no love scenes.' Those are certain guidelines I don't think I can stretch."*[6]

A NASTY FIGHT ON THE PLAYGROUND

Years before agreeing to make *Space Jam*, Jordan had negotiated a deal to be part of a 1991 basketball-themed movie called *Heaven Is a Playground*. He backed out before it went into production, and without Jordan as leading man, the movie was not distributed nationally and earned a meager $168,000.

The filmmakers of that failed film later sued Jordan for breach of contract; Jordan filed a countersuit claiming the producers falsely represented they had lined up financing. On October 15, 1998, a Chicago jury ruled in favor of Jordan, finding that the producers misled Jordan into believing there was sufficient financing for the film. Jurors also awarded him $50,000 in compensatory damages, the amount of the fee he had originally received from Heaven Corp. and later returned.

Dean Dickie, attorney for the plaintiffs, knew from the outset he faced an uphill battle. He said that trying the Bulls basketball star in Chicago was like "trying God in Heaven." After the case concluded, the jurors asked Jordan to autograph their jury service certificates, although they insisted his fame had no bearing on their decision.

Jordan said afterward he felt vindicated, adding:

"I felt like someone was trying to attack my integrity."[7]

THE JORDAN END GAME

In the first part of the 1988–89 season, Michael Jordan played an average of 40.4 minutes per game, more than anyone else in the league. Other players speculated that Jordan soon would wear out. But not Jordan.

"Hey, I'm a young thoroughbred, and young thoroughbreds don't need rest."[1]

Eventually, however, Jordan did get tired. The first time weariness set in was after the original three championship seasons. The situation was exacerbated by the emotional devastation caused by the death of his father. The next episode of mental exhaustion came after Jordan again led the Chicago Bulls to a three-peat championship. Perhaps he'd seen the specter of aging; perhaps he was dispirited at the thought of working through a looming NBA labor dispute; perhaps he couldn't face any of these things without the inspiration of Coach Jackson, who would be resigning at the end of the season.

"I think that even with Phil as coach, I would have had a tough time mentally finding the challenge for myself, although he could somehow present challenges for me. I don't know if he could have presented a challenge for me to continue on with this season—even though midway through the season [1997–98] I wanted to continue to play a couple more years. But at the end of the season, I was mentally drained and tired."[2]

~

Jordan, for the second time, considered retirement. Chicago Bulls primary owner Jerry Reinsdorf said he had known since the Bulls won the 1998 championship that Michael Jordan was unlikely to return for an encore season. "He said he never was so tired in his life," recalled Reinsdorf. "He said it was his hardest year, and he felt he had to carry the team in the finals more than he'd ever had. He was totally exhausted, mentally and physically."[3]

FEAR OF AGING

Jordan began worrying about not being able to maintain the standards he set for himself long before he retired. After winning three straight NBA scoring titles, Jordan, at the time 29 years old, said he felt he had to maintain his performance and score an average of 32 points a game.

"If I have 22 points a game, I've had a bad year. I've set my standards so high now that I've got to maintain that consistency. If I don't, I'm at the point in my career where people will start saying, 'Maybe he's getting old' or 'Maybe he's on his way out.'"[4]

After his NBA comeback in 1995, Jordan realized he was no longer the young thoroughbred of the late 1980s, but he wasn't ready to be put out to pasture either. He compensated for any age-induced loss of agility by working on solid moves, such as the turn-around jumpshot, and his famous fall-away jumper. They were not quite as acrobatic or daring as his earlier feats of flight, but nevertheless scored points and rattled, then defeated, his opponents.

"I may not look as flamboyant as I was in the past, but the end result is basically the same. It's not always how you look—it's how you achieve."[5]

By the 1998 playoffs, sportswriters noted that Bulls were senior citizens by NBA standards. Jordan, their head guard, was 35 at the time. Jordan retorted with this comment:

"Yeah, we're old. We're probably the oldest team in the league. That means that we are the most experienced, too. We know what to expect and how to get around some of the potholes."[6]

~

During the 1998 NBA championship series pitting the veteran Chicago Bulls against the Utah Jazz, also a relatively "old" team, Jordan raised hopes by saying he felt strong enough to play another season.

"I feel good. As long as you give me time enough to prepare myself for the grueling season, physically work out and get myself in shape, I'm not worried about playing a whole season, a couple of seasons, whatever."[7]

~

His level of fitness left no room for doubt when he led the East to a 135–114 victory over the West in the 1998 All-Star game. Days before his 35th birthday, Jordan declared himself at the top of his game. If anything, he said, experience gained over the years enhanced his skills.

"I'm the best basketball player I can be right now. My game has elevated from just the slam-dunker I was when I came in the league. A lot of this has come with my maturity, making the plays."[8]

~

Jordan staved off the effects of aging with the help of a personal trainer and a rigorous year-round conditioning program. He had a gym and a weight room built into his Highland Park, Illinois, estate.

"I've taken the physical strengthening of my body seriously. Before this stage, I had my youth to live

off and rely upon. Now it's not quite the same. As you grow older, the body starts giving you signals that you [have] got to listen to and do the things that are correct. I just feel that physically I've got to be in the best shape possible to be able to consistently do my job."[9]

When it was reported that Jordan had his home gym torn out and remodeled it into a cigar bar, fans took it as an early warning sign that he would indeed retire before the 1999 season.

∼

Jordan wanted to time his departure carefully. In 1998, he said:

"If you want to leave the game, you don't want to leave the game limping. You want to leave with you still knowing, and the people knowing, you could play two more years."[10]

IF THE COACH GOES, SO DO I

Bulls general manager Jerry Krause—no fan of Coach Phil Jackson (and the bad feelings were mutual)—had warned the coach that the 1997–98 season would be his last with the Bulls.

Before the season began, Jackson told reporters: "Jerry and I sat down and had a talk. He wanted to make sure there wasn't any discussion that came up this day that would leave the door open for me to come back to this particular organization. I assured him my intent was to walk out at the end of this season and he assisted me in that belief."[11]

～

The strongest reason to believe Michael Jordan's career was nearing an end was his oft-repeated statement that he would never play for a coach other than Phil Jackson. If Jackson left the team, so would Jordan. He said:

"I won't play. I'll retire. It is that simple. I won't play anywhere else, I won't follow Phil. I will totally retire. That clears up every question. What management is saying, if Phil is out, then this is my last year."[12]

～

Following a game at Toronto, Jordan repeated his statement but made it more ambivalent, raising his fans' hopes again.

"I would still love to play for Phil and still in Chicago. But I won't play anywhere else, and I won't play for anyone else but Phil."[13]

And if the Bulls did not retain Jackson for the next season, did that mean he would be essentially forced off the team? Not really, replied Jordan:

"It's never forced as long as I have a choice."[14]

～

Jordan could not resist leaving the door open to the possibility of another season or two. He kept everyone guessing:

> *"I'm happy that I have a choice. I have a choice to either play or not play. Very few athletes get in this position where they have a choice to either play or not play. That's the happy part about Michael Jordan. It might be confusing, but someday you will sit back and sort it out."[15]*

~

Jordan's resolve to leave deepened when an Iowa State University coach, Tim Floyd, was rumored to have been selected as Phil Jackson's replacement. Nothing personal, Jordan insisted. He was simply too far along in his career to have to adapt to a new coaching style:

> *"I don't know Tim Floyd. I don't have anything against Tim Floyd. Having a new coach is like starting out all over again."[16]*

~

Jordan's best friend in the NBA, Houston Rocket Charles Barkley, said in the summer of 1998—months before Jordan's official retirement announcement—that hopes that Jordan would stay were nothing more than wishful thinking. Jordan, Barkley said, had made up his mind: "Michael is done. You can hope and hope and hope, but Michael is gone. He's not coming back because he's fed up with the way the Bulls have disrespected his wishes and disrespected him. Here is a man who made it clear to the world that he wouldn't play for any coach but Phil Jackson. So what do the Bulls do? They chase Phil away, hire another coach [Tim Floyd], and then ask Phil to come back when they knew he wouldn't."[17]

THE LAST GREAT SEASON

When Jordan returned back in 1995, it reenergized the Bulls and his fans and the league in general. But it also led to another round of speculation: How long would Jordan's second incarnation last? Jordan's potential retirement was expected to have serious consequences for televised professional basketball. The star's drawing power made Chicago Bulls games the hottest commodity for NBC and Turner Sports.

During the 1997–98 season, NBC, which had exclusive NBA broadcasting rights, reported an average 6.5 Nielsen rating when Jordan and the Chicago Bulls played. The average rating fell 69 percent to 3.8 when other team games were televised.

Variety reported that for the rights to broadcast NBA games under a four-year license fee, NBC increased the amount it paid from $750 million in the seasons between 1994 and 1998 to $1.75 billion for the seasons between 1998 and 2003.[18]

In December 1997, Jordan denied rumors that he would play another season to satisfy a provision in the deal the NBA renegotiated for broadcast rights with

NBC, TBS, and TNT. But even if he had stayed for another season or two, he said it was unrealistic to think he alone could rescue the league from years of conflicts over salary limits and other troubles.

"One person can't solve a multitude of problems. Basketball now is starting to show cracks that are going to spread if you don't take care of them. Once you get a crack in the armor, believe me, the whole armor is in danger. It gets magnified. It starts to spread and people look at the littlest things in the largest ways."[19]

During his last season, Jordan still was intent on living and playing in the present:

"I don't want a tour. I don't want to do anything. If it's the end, it's the end. I don't want to remind myself this is the end. I enjoy each and every moment, each and every city I play [in], knowing it could very well be the last time."[20]

During the 1997–98 season, fans packed stadiums across the country to witness what they feared might be the denouement of the Chicago Bulls dynasty. At a game in Atlanta in March 1998, a record 62,046 came to watch the Bulls play the Hawks, breaking an NBA attendance record. People paid hundreds of dollars for standing-room space, from which they couldn't even see the court. Jordan said:

"I think the feeling people have this year is that it's going to end. And I think they should enjoy it, because you never know when it's all going to be taken away."[21]

~

During the Bulls' heyday, the team's warehouse was filled with gifts. People sent Bibles, oil paintings of Jordan, curtains, bathrobes, and food, among other items. During what proved to be their last season, the Bulls received about 6,000 pieces a month for Jordan from around the world, including money for photos or tickets (all of which was returned to senders).

"They're desperate to get to him before he retires," said Jackie Banks, who handled Jordan's mail.[22]

~

When Jordan secured the win for the Bulls in the final seconds of the 1998 championships with a jump shot, it formed a perfect arc of triumph. But would it prove to be his last shot ever as an NBA player?

THE NBA LOCKOUT

The NBA salary dispute began June 30, 1998, not long after the Bulls celebrated their sixth "ring" in eight years. It was settled during a marathon negotiating session January 6, on the eve of the deadline for canceling the season. The following day, the league's board of governors voted 29–0 to ratify a new contract with the players.[23]

Bulls chairman Jerry Reinsdorf awaited word from Jordan, telling the media that the Bulls management would make no major decisions until Jordan said whether he would stay or go. Reinsdorf told *Chicago Tribune* columnist Sam Smith that he had made one last unsuccessful effort to get Phil Jackson to return as coach, but Jackson stood fast.

"He [Jackson] always told me he wasn't going to coach [this season]," Reinsdorf said. "But people change their minds. I wanted to be sure. I figured he had the summer off; he looked pretty good on TV, his beard was gone, he looked younger. I figured he had the itch again. That's why I called him."[24]

∼

Michael Jordan chose to retire when the lockout ended, and Scottie Pippen and Dennis Rodman became free agents, eventually going to other teams. What would the Chicago Bulls be like after its dynasty dissolved?

Jordan thought he caught a peek at the future when his team got off to a slow start in the 1997–98 season. With Scottie Pippen injured and team members exhausted because their charter flight had been delayed six hours for repairs, the Bulls lost their game against the Cleveland Cavaliers by 21 points.

After the game, Jordan commented:

"I'll tell you, it gives Chicago [a glimpse of] the coming years, huh?"[25]

THE CLAMOROUS GOODBYE

On January 5, 1999, hours before NBA negotiators reached agreement on a contract, NBA commissioner David Stern was asked on CNN's *Larry King Live* whether having Michael Jordan continue to play was essential to rebuilding the lockout-crippled league.

Stern hesitated to say yes. "You know, I don't want to hurt his feelings," he said. "We would love to have him back, and it would make things much easier, but he is actually going to retire someday, and I think there are a great number of young players."

But King persisted. Wouldn't Stern rather have Jordan play than not play?

"Do you want to see me beg right here?" asked Stern.

"Yes, please," replied King.

Stern looked directly into the television camera. "Michael, if you're watching, please, Michael, come back. Tell us you'll come back."[26]

∼

The day before Jordan made his departure official, ESPN ran highlights of Jordan's career to the sounds of a choir solemnly, reverently singing "Amen." Jordan's retirement led the news around the world, and *Newsweek* featured Jordan on its cover. The coverage of his retirement press conference January 13, 1999, eclipsed the impending impeachment trial of President Clinton.

Sports programs worldwide ran hours and hours of

Michael Jordan specials and retrospectives. ESPN Classic Sports Network offered 56 straight hours of programming on the basketball star.

The extent of the coverage prompted John Maffei, a sports media writer for the San Diego *North County Times*, to grumble, "He didn't die, and he wasn't a god or a president. All the hype is just a little out of whack."[27]

~

Hall of Fame running back Jim Brown, who also retired in his prime at 29, applauded Jordan for choosing the right time to leave basketball.

"It's a brilliant decision," he said. "The man created a miracle last year. You can never top yourself. Once it becomes you versus you, the older you is going to lose."[28]

~

When Michael hung up his Air Jordans, sportswriters reflected on the mental and emotional pressures the superstar had suffered at center stage. The *San Diego Union-Tribune*'s Tom Cushman wrote that "We've been smothering him. All of us—fans, media, predators. We've crowded around until there [was] no breathing room.

"It's what we do to superstars these days. Why should it be surprising that a celestial presence like Michael felt himself beginning to suffocate. We were killing him with love."[29]

THE JORDAN LEGACY

Jordan summarized his own legacy this way:

"I played it to the best that I could play it. I tried to enhance the game itself. I've tried to be the best basketball player I could be. And next thing you know, here we are as a league. I think the league is going to continue on although we've had our troubles over the last six months. I think that's a reality check for all of us. It is a business but yet it's still fun, it's still a game, and the game will continue on."[30]

~

Dean Smith, Jordan's college coach at the University of North Carolina, said, "I think when all this is done, Michael's place in the history of basketball will be clear. Very, very, very clear."[31]

~

A statue in front of the United Center in Chicago is inscribed, "Michael Jordan Chicago Bulls 1984–1993 [soon to be updated to reflect his comeback years, 1995–1998]. The best there ever was. The best there ever will be."

~

Charles Barkley, as always, was more pragmatic. As early as 1989, he stated he had no doubt that professional basketball would go forward, no matter what he or Jordan or anyone else did. And as Michael Jordan says, you can count on Barkley to tell the truth.

"There will be another Michael Jordan, another Larry Bird, another Charles Barkley. God is so good to us. If someone told you five years ago a 6-foot 4-inch, 250-pound guy would lead the league in rebounding, you'd say I was full of shit. If someone told you there'd be a 6-foot 10-inch guy from Nigeria, Hakeem Olajuwon, who could outrun guards, you wouldn't believe it. If someone told there'd be a white guy 5-foot-whatever who could play like John Stockton, you wouldn't believe that either. They just keep coming."[32]

POSTSCRIPT

"My responsibility has been to play the game of basketball and relieve some of the pressure of everyday life for people who work from 9 to 5, and I've tried to do that to the best of my abilities."[33]

~

When Jordan retired for the second time, just a month before his 36th birthday, he did not go into detail about his future career plans. Instead, he focused on his family duties, and his opportunity to spend more time with his three children.

"Being a parent is very challenging. If you have kids you know that. I welcome that challenge, and I look forward to it."[34]

~

"I will live vicariously through my kids as they play the game of basketball. If they don't, I will support that."[35]

∽

Asked how Jordan's retirement would affect her life, his wife Juanita said, "My life won't change at all. I see Michael doing more carpooling."[36]

∽

Asked at his retirement press conference if he planned to solve the world's problems, Jordan replied:

"I don't think I can go into seclusion. I will still be doing commercials, but I can't save the world, by no means."[37]

∽

It is clear what Jordan did not want to do: He said he did not want to own the Bulls or work for the team in any capacity other than as a player.[38]

In November 1997, Jordan told CBS Sportsline that he could not imagine himself coaching or managing an NBA team, at least not until time had mellowed him.

"I really don't have the patience for any of that right now. I know me. I'm too competitive. I hold such high standards, I couldn't be patient with players developing. I'm too close to it."[39]

∽

Whatever path his life follows now, Jordan will maintain the supreme self-confidence that he's gained from succeeding at basketball:

> *"Confidence allows you to progress in something you're attempting to accomplish, whether it's playing basketball or baseball, or whether it's trying to succeed in business."*[40]

∿

When Michael Jordan appeared on *The Keenan Ivory Wayans Show* during the 1998 basketball season, he described one vision of his future.

> *"And one day, this is going to sound wild, but my ultimate dream is to get a pot belly. I know it sounds bad and everything, but I've always had to stay focused and stay in shape."*[41]

∿

Several months after his retirement, Jordan participated in an online chat room on America Online CBS Sportsline. When asked what retirement was like, he replied:

> *"You just wake up [every day] and try to figure out what it means. I just want to use this time to enjoy my life."*

But, added Jordan, there was already one benefit from retirement:

> *"I get to drop [my kids] off at school and attend their basketball games."*[42]

~

Chicago Tribune columnist Bob Greene, who wrote two books about Jordan, warned the superstar that his public image was too powerful to ever escape from:

> *"You can retire from the Bulls and the NBA, but you can never retire from being Michael Jordan."*[43]

BY THE NUMBERS

NORTH CAROLINA

	G	FG%	FT%	Reb	Ast	Stl	Points	PPG
1981–82	34	.534	.722	149	61	41	460	13.5
1982–83	36	.535	.737	197	56	78	721	20.0
1983–84	31	.551	.779	163	64	50	607	19.6
TOTAL	101	.540	.748	509	181	169	1,788	17.7

NBA REGULAR SEASON

Year	G	FG%	FT%	Reb	Ast	Stl	Pt	PPG
1984–85	82	.515	.845	534	481	196	2,313	28.2
1985–86	18	.457	.840	64	53	37	408	22.7
1986–87	82	.482	.857	430	377	236	3,041	37.1
1987–88	82	.535	.841	449	485	259	2,868	35.0
1988–89	81	.538	.850	652	650	234	2,633	32.5
1989–90	82	.526	.848	565	519	227	2,753	33.6
1990–91	82	.539	.851	492	453	223	2,580	31.5
1991–92	80	.519	.832	511	489	182	2,404	30.1
1992–93	78	.495	.837	522	428	221	2,541	32.6
1994–95	17	.411	.801	117	90	30	457	26.9
1995–96	82	.495	.834	543	352	180	2,491	30.4
1996–97	82	.486	.833	482	352	140	2,431	29.6
1997–98	82	.465	.784	475	283	141	2,357	28.7
TOTALS	930	.505	.838	5,836	5,012	2,306	29,277	31.5

NBA POST-SEASON

Year	G	FG%	FT%	Reb	Ast	Stl	Pts	PPG
1984–85	4	.436	.828	23	34	11	117	29.3
1985–86	3	.505	.872	19	17	7	131	43.7
1986–87	3	.417	.897	21	18	6	107	35.7
1987–88	10	.531	.869	71	47	24	363	36.3
1988–89	17	.510	.799	119	130	42	591	34.8
1989–90	16	.514	.836	115	109	45	587	36.7
1990–91	17	.524	.845	108	142	40	529	31.1
1991–92	22	.499	.857	137	127	44	759	34.5
1992–93	19	.475	.805	128	114	39	666	35.1
1994–95	10	.484	.810	65	45	23	315	31.5
1995–96	18	.459	.818	89	74	33	552	30.7
1996–97	19	.456	.831	150	91	30	590	31.1
1997–98	21	.462	.812	107	74	32	680	32.4
TOTALS	179	.487	.828	1,158	1,022	376	5,987	33.4

KEY

G = number of games
FG% = percent of successful field goals
FT% = percent of successful free throws
Reb = number of rebounds
Ast = number of assists
Pts = number of points
PPG = average points per game
Stl = steals

OTHER CAREER HIGHLIGHTS

NBA Most Valuable Player	5
NBA Finals Most Valuable Player	6
Finals MVP	6
Member NBA Championship Team (Chicago Bulls)	6
NBA Scoring Titles	10
All-Star	11 (named to a 12th but did not play because of a broken foot)
Defensive First Team	9
Slam-Dunk Champion	1987, 1988
Career Average Points per Game	31.5 (NBA record as of 1998)
Average Points per All-Star Game	21.3 (NBA record as of 1998)
Highest Points Scored in a Regular Season Game	69 (March 28, 1990, in Bulls' 117–113 overtime win over Cleveland Cavaliers)
Highest Points Scored in a Playoff Game	63 (April 20, 1986, in loss to Boston Celtics in double overtime)
Number of Game-Winning Shots	25
Regular Season and Playoff Games, 50 or more points scored	37
Member, winning U.S. Olympic basketball team	1984, 1992
Seasons with 2,000 points or more	11

CHICAGO BULLS

SEASON	WINS	LOSSES	
1980–81	45	37	
1981–82	19	32	
1982–83	28	54	
1983–84	27	55	
1984–85	38	44	(Jordan's rookie year. First time Bulls reach playoffs since 1981)
1985–86	30	52	(Jordan played only 18 games due to broken foot)
1986–87	40	42	
1987–88	50	32	
1988–89	47	35	
1989–90	55	27	
1990–91	61	21	
1991–92	67	15	
1992–93	57	25	
1993–94	55	27	(Jordan did not play)
1994–95	47	35	(Jordan returned to NBA in midseason, playing only 17 games)
1995–96	72	10	
1996–97	69	13	
1997–98	62	20	

NOTE: Data compiled from multiple sources.

TIMELINE

1963 *February 17:* Michael Jeffrey Jordan was born to Deloris and James Jordan in Brooklyn, New York, where his father was taking vocational courses. He was the fourth of the family's five children. The Jordans returned to North Carolina later that year, living first in James's hometown of Wallace, later settling in nearby Wilmington, where Michael grew up and attended school.

1975 The Dixie Youth Association named Michael Jordan "Mr. Baseball" among North Carolina's 12-year-olds. Jordan excelled at Little League baseball. He played shortstop and pitcher.

1978 Jordan was devastated when he failed to make the varsity basketball team at Emsley A. Laney High School. He played baseball during two full high school seasons and part of his senior year. He made the Laney Buccaneers varsity basketball team his junior year, and played as a senior. Jordan led his team to its first conference victory.

1980 Between his junior and senior year in high school, Michael Jordan attended Dean Smith's basketball camp at the University of North Carolina, Chapel Hill, where his burgeoning talent was recognized by Smith's assistant, Roy Williams. Later Jordan went to the Five Star Camp in Pittsburgh, Pennsylvania.

Something of an unknown among high school athletes, Jordan dazzled the other players and coaches, winning honors as Most Valuable Player of the league and MVP of the All-Star game.

1981 Jordan graduated from Laney as a good college basketball prospect. He opted to go to top-ranked North Carolina, where respected coach Dean Smith helped develop both Jordan's basketball skills and his self-discipline.

1982 *March 29:* Jordan made his first impression on the national sports consciousness when he lead his Tar Heels to an NCAA title victory against Georgetown by scoring on a jump shot with 17 seconds left on the clock.

1983 Jordan was named *Sporting News'* Player of the Year.

1984 After his third season with the Tar Heels, Jordan was named the *Sporting News'* Player of the Year for the second year in a row and captured the Naismith and Wooden awards. He left North Carolina after his junior year.

June: The Chicago Bulls picked Jordan in the NBA draft. He was the third selection; the first was Hakeem Olajuwon, who went to Houston; second was Sam Bowie, who went to Portland.

August: The summer prior to entering the pros, Jordan co-captained the 1984 U.S. Olympic basketball team, which won the gold medal at the Olympic Games in Los Angeles.

1985 Jordan capped his first season with the Bulls as the NBA's Rookie of the Year. He played in his first All-Star game.

October 29: Jordan broke a bone in his left foot during the third game of the season.

1986 Despite being on the disabled list for 64 games in the 1985–86 season, fans voted Jordan to the All-Star team.

1987 Jordan scored a total of 3,041 points, higher than any other guard and the third highest in NBA history for a single season.

Jordan won the NBA's Slam-Dunk competition.

Jordan named to the first All-NBA team.

1988 Jordan named the NBA's Most Valuable Player and Defensive Player of the Year.

He was again named to All-NBA first team and All-Defensive team, a double honor repeated the following year.

Jordan won second consecutive Slam-Dunk championship.

Juanita and Michael's first son, Jeffrey, was born.

Jordan signed his second contract with the Chicago Bulls, for $25 million over eight years.

1989 Jordan won the IBM Award for his team contributions.

September 2: Jordan married Juanita Vanoy, a former executive secretary for the American Bar Association, in the Little White Wedding Chapel in Las Vegas. The couple honeymooned in La Costa, California, where Jordan liked to golf.

1990 *January 26:* Jordan surpassed former Bull Bob Love's record for total number of points, 12,623, in a game against Philadelphia. Jordan scored 31 points that night.

March 28: In a Bulls victory over Cleveland, Jordan scored 69 points and made 18 rebounds.

1991 *November:* The publication of the book *The Jordan Rules*, by the *Chicago Tribune*'s Sam Smith, presented some negative views of Jordan's relations with other Bulls players and stirred a public controversy.

June: Jordan's Bulls won their first NBA championship, defeating the Los Angeles Lakers in five games. Jordan was named Most Valuable Player in the Finals. The previous month, he had been named NBA Most Valuable Player for the second consecutive year.

1992 *February:* After Jordan won a licensing dispute with the NBA, the league was no longer allowed to use Jordan's likeness in promotion and advertising.

Jordan named NBA Most Valuable Player for the third time and led the Bulls to their second NBA championship.

August: Jordan won a second Olympic gold medal as a member of the U.S. basketball squad, known as the Dream Team, during the Olympic Summer Games in Barcelona, Spain. Dean Smith, Jordan's college mentor, coached the team.

October 23: In the drug and money-laundering trial of his former golfing partner James Bouler, Jordan was a witness, testifying that he lost $57,000 to Bouler in gambling debts. Initially, Jordan said the $57,000 check was a loan to Bouler.

1993 *May 26:* A *New York Times* story disclosed that Jordan was seen gambling in an Atlantic City, New Jersey, casino following a playoff game the Bulls lost to the New York Knickerbockers. He and the Bulls rallied in later games and defeated the Knicks to advance in the playoffs.

June 3: Concerns over Jordan's gambling flared anew when Richard Esquinas, a golfing partner and former president of the San Diego Sports Arena, self-published a book titled *Michael & Me: Our*

Gambling Addiction, My Cry for Help. Esquinas alleged that Jordan ran up $1.25 million in gambling debts on their golf games. Jordan said the figure was grossly exaggerated.

June 11: The NBA ruled that Jordan's gambling had not violated league regulations.

June 20: The Chicago Bulls won their third consecutive NBA championship defeating the Phoenix Suns.

July 23: James Jordan, Michael's father, was murdered in his car parked off a North Carolina road late at night. He was returning to his home in Charlotte after attending the funeral of a friend.

October 6: Jordan announced his retirement from the NBA.

1994 *February 7:* Jordan signed a free-agent contract with the Chicago White Sox. The following month he was assigned to the team's Double-A affiliate.

April 8: Jordan debuted with the Double-A Birmingham Barons. During his 127 games, he batted .202.

November 1: Jordan's jersey was retired during a ceremony at the Bulls' new United Center. Outside, a 12-foot bronze statue of Jordan was unveiled.

1995 *March 19:* Jordan resumed his NBA career, playing his first game with the Bulls against the Indiana Pacers.

June: Jordan joined the effort to decertify the NBA Players Association as the bargaining unit for players.

1996 Jordan led the Bulls back to supremacy. The team finished the regular season with a record-making 72–10, the best in NBA history. The team captured its fourth NBA championship by defeating Seattle in the finals.

The live-action/cartoon *Space Jam*, Jordan's first Hollywood feature film, was released.

Jordan, along with Mel Gibson and Jerry Seinfeld, was named *GQ's* man of the year.

1997 Jordan was named one of the NBA's 50 greatest all-time players.

June: The Bulls beat the Utah Jazz in the finals to win their fifth NBA title.

Jordan named *Sporting News'* Most Powerful Person in Sports.

November 30: Jordan scored his 25,000th career point, on his last play in a game against the San Antonio Spurs.

1998 Jordan won his tenth NBA scoring title, averaging 28.7 points. He won MVP honor at his twelfth All-Star game. He was named All-Defensive First Team for the ninth time.

June: The Bulls again defeated the Utah Jazz in the NBA finals, giving the Bulls their sixth NBA championship. Jordan was again chosen MVP, his sixth finals MVP award.

Jordan was named the league's Most Valuable Player for the fifth time.

The NBA lockout delayed the start of the 1998–99 season. NBA players tried to negotiate a settlement with team owners over salary caps.

1999 *January 6:* NBA lockout ended. The sports world anxiously awaited word from Jordan as to whether he would play in the shortened 52-game season.

January 13: Michael Jordan announced his retirement from the NBA.

ENDNOTES

Preface

1. "Letters," *Time*, July 13, 1998.

2. Wayne Friedman, "Jordan the Star Athlete Retires, Jordan the Brand Comes to Life," *Advertising Age*, January 18, 1999, p. 3.

3. Steve Marantz, "The Power of Air," *Sporting News*, December 22, 1997, p. 12.

4. Charles P. Pierce, "Michael Jordan: A Revolutionary But No Rebel, He Changed the Game and Left the World Alone," *GQ*, November 1996, p. 324.

5. Allen Barra, "A Fawning New Book on Michael Jordan Scores Points for Flattery," *Wall Street Journal*, January 22, 1999, p. W1.

6. Jeff Coplon, "Legends. Champions?" *New York Times Magazine*, April 21, 1996, p. 32.

7. Terry Mulgannon, "Giving Back," *Sports*, December 1993, p. 38.

8. Joel Achenbach, "'This is a Perfect Time for Me to Walk Away,'" *Washington Post*, January 15, 1999.

A Little Hardship Early

1. Michael Jordan, *For the Love of the Game: My Story* (New York: Crown Publishers, Inc., 1998), p. 13.

2. Bob Sakamoto, "Family Is at the Core of Jordan's Dream," *Chicago Tribune*, April 15, 1990.

3. Deloris Jordan, *Family First: Winning the Parenting Game* (New York: Harper San Francisco, 1996), pp. 24–25.

4. Bob Sakamoto, "Family Is at the Core of Jordan's Dream," *Chicago Tribune*, April 15, 1990.

5. Jim Naughton, *Taking to the Air* (New York: Warner Books, 1992), p. 42.

6. Mark Vancil, "Michael Jordan (interview)," *Playboy*, May 1992, p. 51.

7. Michael Jordan, *Rare Air* (San Francisco: Collins Publishers San Francisco, 1993), p. 69.

8. Deloris Jordan, *Family First: Winning the Parenting Game* (New York: Harper San Francisco, 1996), p. 18.

9. Renee Stovsky, "Michael's Mom Deloris Jordan Raised a Son, Not a Superstar," *St. Louis Post-Dispatch*, July 31, 1996, p. 1E.

10. David Breskin, "Michael Jordan: The Best There Ever Was," *GQ*, March 1989, p. 323.

11. Michael Krugel, *Jordan, His Words, His Life* (New York: St. Martin's Press, 1994), p. 227.

12. Michael Jordan, *For the Love of the Game: My Story* (New York: Crown Publishers, Inc., 1998), p. 138.

13. Karen M. Thomas, "She Taught Mike What to Be Like," *Dallas Morning News*, August 21, 1996, p. 1C.

14. "Air Time: Kids Ask Michael Jordan about Hoops and Life," *Sports Illustrated for Kids*, March 1996, p. 32.

15. "Mike on Mike (Allison Samuels interview with Michael Jordan)," *Newsweek*, September 22, 1997, p. 70.

16. Bob Greene, *Hang Time* (New York: Doubleday, 1992), p. 87.

17. Curry Kirkpatrick, "A Towering Twosome," *Sports Illustrated*, November 28, 1983, p. 52.

18. Bob Greene, *Hang Time* (New York: Doubleday, 1992), p. 45.

19. Renee Stovsky, "Michael's Mom Deloris Jordan Raised a Son, Not a Superstar," *St. Louis Post-Dispatch*, July 31, 1996, p. 1E.

20. Michael Jordan, *Rare Air* (San Francisco: Collins Publishers San Francisco, 1993), p. 105.

21. Michael Jordan, Sportsline, America Online, March 22, 1999.

22. Bob Sakamoto, "Family Is at the Core of Jordan's Dream,"*Chicago Tribune*, April 15, 1990.

23. Michael Jordan, *For the Love of the Game: My Story* (New York: Crown Publishers, Inc., 1998), p. 95.

The Tar Heel

1. Curry Kirkpatrick, "A Towering Twosome," *Sports Illustrated*, November 28, 1983, p. 52.

2. Ibid.

3. David Halberstam, "Becoming Michael Jordan," Excerpted from "Michael Jordan: The Making of a Legend," *Vanity Fair*, October 1998, p. 132.

4. Alexander Wolff, "Sportsman of the Year: Dean Smith Unplugged," *Sports Illustrated*, December 22, 1997.

5. A.J. Carr, "UNC Tops Jayhawks in Opener," *Raleigh News and Observer*," November 28, 1981.

6. Mike Kiley, "Pluck, Luck Put UNC on Top," *Chicago Tribune*, March 30, 1982.

7. Curry Kirkpatrick, "The Heels Are Alive and Kicking," *Sports Illustrated*, January 17, 1983, p. 30.

8. Ibid.

9. Alexander Wolff, "Sportsman of the Year: Dean Smith Unplugged," *Sports Illustrated*, December 22, 1997.

10. Curry Kirkpatrick, "A Towering Twosome," *Sports Illustrated*, November 28, 1983, p. 52.

11. Ibid.

12. Barry Jacobs, "High-Flying Michael Jordan Has North Carolina Cruising toward Another NCAA Title," *People Weekly*, March 29, 1984, p. 42.

13. Kent McDill, "School Days Are Here Again for Jordan," www:CBS Sportsline.com, March 15, 1998.

14. Michael Jordan (audio). "1997 Sportsman of the Year," www.cnnsi.com.

15. Michael Jordan, *Rare Air* (San Francisco: Collins Publishers San Francisco, 1993), p. 32.

16. Alexander Wolff, "1997 Sportsman of the Year," www.cnnsi.com.

17. Ibid.

18. Ivan Maisel, "College Basketball: Famous N.C. Alumnus Needs No Introduction," *Newsday*, January 11, 1995.

19. Barry Jacobs, "High-Flying Michael Jordan Has North Carolina Cruising toward Another NCAA Title," *People Weekly*, March 19, 1984, p. 42.

20. Bob Logan, "Bulls Hope Jordan Is a Savior," *Chicago Tribune*, June 17, 1984.

21. Renee Stovsky, "Michael's Mom Deloris Jordan Raised a Son, Not a Superstar," *St. Louis Post-Dispatch*, July 31, 1996, p. 1E.

22. David Halberstam, "Becoming Michael Jordan," Excerpted from "Michael Jordan: The Making of a Legend," *Vanity Fair*, October 1998, p. 146.

The NBA's Lord of the Hoops

1. Mark Vancil, "Eighteen Times a Rare Silver Dollar Had Been Flipped into the Air," *Sports Illustrated*, July 7, 1993, p. 16.

2. Ibid.

3. Bob Logan, "Jordan Joins Youth Movement," *Chicago Tribune*, June 20, 1984.

4. Terry Boers, "Here Comes Mr. Jordan," *Hoop Magazine*, January, 1985, www.nba.com/mjretirement.

5. Ibid.

6. Ibid.

7. "Air Time: Kids Ask Michael Jordan About Hoops and Life," *Sports Illustrated for Kids*, March 1996, p. 32.

8. Bob Sakamoto, "A Bullish Beginning for MJ," *Chicago Tribune*, October 27, 1984.

9. Alexander Wolff, "In the Driver's Seat," *Sports Illustrated*, December 10, 1984, p. 36.

10. Ibid.

11. Bob Sakamoto, "In the End, Jordan's No. 1, *Chicago Tribune*, March 17, 1985.

12. Rick Telander, "Ready . . . Set . . . Levitate! Midair is the Lofty Realm of Chicago's Michael Jordan, and He Has Lifted the Bulls Off to a Stratospheric Start," *Sports Illustrated*, November 17, 1986, p. 16.

13. Elliott Harris, "Sixth Sense of a Superstar: A 6-Pack of MJ Highlights," *Chicago Sun-Times Online*, January 12, 1999.

14. Craig Neff and Robert Sullivan, "Air Jordan Has No Fear of Flying," *Sports Illustrated*, March 24, 1986, p. 10.

15. Roland Lazenby, *And Now, Your Chicago Bulls!* (Dallas, TX: Taylor Publishing Co., 1995), p. 149.

16. Henry Louis Gates Jr., "Net Worth: How the Greatest Player in the History of Basketball Became the Greatest Brand in the History of Sports," *New Yorker*, June 1, 1998, p. 48.

17. Michael Jordan, *For the Love of the Game: My Story* (New York: Crown Publishers, Inc., 1998), p. 28.

18. Marty Burns, "Jordanalia," *Sports Illustrated*, January 20, 1999, p. 8.

19. "Jordan: NBA at 50 Interview, Part I" www.nba.com/mjretirement, 1999.

20. Ibid.

21. Melissa Isaacson, "Jordan Is Irritated as Chicago Continues Slide into Mediocrity," *St. Louis Post-Dispatch*, February 2, 1993, p. 5B.

22. "Jordan: NBA at 50 Interview, Part 1," www.nba.com/mjretirement, 1999.

23. Bob Greene, *Hang Time* (New York: Doubleday, 1992), p. 327.

24. Mike Lupica, "Hoop Dreaming," *Esquire*, November 1, 1996.

25. Jim O'Donnell, "The Stuff of an NBA Legend," *Chicago Sun-Times*, January 13, 1999.

26. Ibid.

27. Michael Jordan, *I Can't Accept Not Trying: Michael Jordan on the Pursuit of Excellence* (San Francisco: Harper San Francisco, 1994), p. 30.

28. Bob Logan, "Bulls Hope Jordan Is a Savior," *Chicago Tribune*, June 17, 1984.

29. Melissa Isaacson, "Head Master," *Sporting News*, April 27, 1998.

30. Barry Jacobs, "High-Flying Michael Jordan Has North Carolina Cruising toward Another NCAA Title," *People Weekly*, March 19, 1984, p. 42.

31. Sam Goldaper, "Jordan Scores 63 in Loss," *New York Times*, April 21, 1986, p. C1.

32. Melissa Isaacson, "The One and Forever Only," *Sporting News*, June 22, 1998, p. 14.

33. Rick Gano, "As Playoffs Start, a Question Tugs at Jordan," AP Online, April 22, 1998.

34. Jack McCallum, "NBA Preview: Mission Impossible," *Sports Illustrated*, November 6, 1989, p. 44.

35. Steve Wulf, "Airing Him Out," *Sports Illustrated*, December 1987, p. 10.

36. Bob Sakamoto, "50-Point Effort Powers Bulls," *Chicago Tribune*, November 2, 1986.

37. Michael Jordan, *Rare Air* (San Francisco: Collins Publishers San Francisco, 1993), p. 53.

38. Curtis Peck, "Morning Briefing," *St. Louis Post-Dispatch*, December 8, 1995, p. 2D.

39. Michael Jordan, *Rare Air* (San Francisco: Collins Publishers San Francisco, 1993), p. 39.

40. Gary Hill, "NBA-Jordan Loves Proving the Doubters Wrong," Reuters, June 8, 1998.

41. Jim Litke, "Jordan Can't Close Door on His Career," *North County Times*, January 14, 1999.

42. Michael Jordan, *Rare Air* (San Francisco: Collins Publishers San Francisco, 1993), p.13.

43. Phil Taylor, "Checking Michael Jordan isn't so strenuous, but it's sure frustrating, says Steve Smith, who did the thankless task for Atlanta," *Sports Illustrated,*" May 19, 1997.

44. Rick Telander, *In the Year of the Bull* (New York: Simon & Schuster, 1996), pp. 139–141.

45. Bob Sakamoto, "Bulls Win 7th Straight," *Chicago Tribune*, April 20, 1988.

46. Charles Barkley with Rick Reilly, *Sir Charles: The Wit and Wisdom of Charles Barkley* (New York: Time Warner Books, 1994), p. 74.

47. Chris Sheridan, "BKN–Jordan's Stare," AP Online, April 30, 1998.

48. Ibid.

Teamwork: The Chicago Bulls

1. Michael Jordan, *I Can't Accept Not Trying: Michael Jordan on the Pursuit of Excellence* (San Francisco: Harper San Francisco, 1994), p. 20.

2. Ibid., pp. 22–23.

3. "Jordan: NBA at 50 Interview, Part 1," www.nba.com/mjretirement, 1999.

4. Phil Jackson and Hugh Delehanty, *Sacred Hoops: Spiritual Lessons of a Hardwood Warrior* (New York: Hyperion, 1995), p. 172.

5. Jack McCallum, "Air Jordan, Air Bulls," *Sports Illustrated*, May 16, 1988, p. 32.

6. Melissa Isaacson, "Jordan Is Irritated as Chicago Continues Slide into Mediocrity," *St. Louis Post-Dispatch*, February 2, 1993, p. 5.

7. Michael Jordan, *For the Love of the Game: My Story* (New York: Crown Publishers, Inc., 1998), p. 93.

8. Sam Smith, *The Jordan Rules* (New York: Simon & Schuster, 1992), p. 249.

9. Michael Jordan, *For the Love of the Game: My Story* (New York: Crown Publishers, Inc., 1998), pp. 40–41.

10. Mitchell Krugel, *Jordan: The Man, His Words, His Life* (New York: St. Martin's Press, 1994), p. 139.

11. Roland Lazenby, *And Now, Your Chicago Bulls!* (Dallas: Taylor Publishing Co., 1995), p.164.

12. Terry Boers, "Here Comes Mr. Jordan," *Hoop Magazine*, January 1985, www.nba.com/mjretirement.

13. Rick Gano, "As Playoff Star, a Question Tugs at Jordan," AP Online, April 22, 1998.

14. Dan Barreiro, "Jordan Shatters Dreams of Rivals," *Minneapolis Star Tribune*, June 15, 1997, p. 1C.

15. "Bulls Wonder, Has the Worm Turned? Jordan Optimistic but Pippen Skeptical about Rodman," *Minneapolis Star Tribune*, October 7, 1995, p. 2C.

16. Dennis Rodman, *Bad As I Wanna Be* (New York: Delacorte Press, 1996), p. 246.

17. Ibid., p. 253.

18. Jeff Coplon, "Legends. Champions?" *New York Times Magazine*, April 21, 1996, p. 54.

19. Steve Aschburner, "Rodman Fined $50,000 for Remarks," *Minneapolis Star Tribune*, June 13, 1997, p. 10C.

20. Kent McDill, "Jordan's Winning Habit," CBS Sportsline, cbs.sportsline.com/I/jordan/offcourt/index.html, December 28, 1997.

21. Kevin Cook, Michael Jordan (interview), *Playboy*, March 1997, p. 122.

22. "Bulls' Jordan Criticizes Rodman's 'Antics' During Playoffs," *Jet*, June 8, 1998, p. 46.

23. Mark Heisler, "Lakers Going Hollyweird," *Los Angeles Times*, February 23, 1999, p. D1.

24. Tim Kawakami, "Rodman Promises He's Back and He Won't Leave Again," *Los Angeles Times*, March 22, 1999, p. D4.

25. Ibid.

26. Bruce Newman, "Black, White—and Gray Piston Dennis Rodman's Life was Complicated by Racial Matters Long Before His Inflammatory Words about Larry Bird," *Sports Illustrated*, May 2, 1988, p. 62.

27. Melissa Isaacson, "More than a Sidekick, Pippen a Partner," *Chicago Tribune*, January 23, 1999.

28. Ibid.

29. Bruce Newman, "Now You See Him: The Bulls' Scottie Pippen Has Leaped from Obscurity to Become a Top NBA Rookie," *Sports Illustrated*, November 30, 1987, p. 67.

30. Ibid.

31. Roland Lazenby, *And Now, Your Chicago Bulls* (Dallas: Taylor Publishing Co., 1995), p. 214.

32. Jack McCallum, "They Are the Insignificant Others of the NBA," *Sports Illustrated*, May 20, 1991, p. 26.

33. Ibid.

34. Gary Hill, "Jordan Campaigns for Return of Bulls, Pippen Casts Doubt," Reuters, June 11, 1998.

35. Ibid.

36. Melissa Isaacson, "More than a Sidekick, Pippen a Partner," *Chicago Tribune*, January 23, 1999.

37. Elliott Harris, "Sixth Sense of a Superstar: A 6-Pack of MJ Highlights," *Chicago Sun-Times Online*, January 12, 1999.

38. Melissa Isaacson, "Second Title Means 'More' to Jordan, *Chicago Tribune*, June 15, 1992.

39. Roland Lazenby, *And Now, Your Chicago Bulls!* (Dallas: Taylor Publishing Co., 1995), p. 223.

40. Melissa Isaacson, "Bulls Shoot for 3: It's Good!" *Chicago Tribune*, June 21, 1993.

41. Terry Armour, "Bulls Prove It: They're the Best," *Chicago Tribune*, June 17, 1996.

42. Steve Wulf, "Mike, and the New Golden Age of Sport. Jordan Again Reminds Us of His Greatness and of How Lucky We Are," *Time*, June 23, 1997.

43. Bonnie DeSimone, "Aw Shucks, Mike, All This for Us? Thanks," *Chicago Tribune*, June 14, 1997.

44. Jeff Ryan, "Champs Again," *Sporting News*, June 22, 1998, p. 10.

45. K.C. Johnson, "Once More, with Feeling," *Chicago Tribune*, June 17, 1998.

46. Harvey Araton, "Let the Trashing Game Begin, *New York Times*, July 23, 1992, p. B17.

47. Ben Kaplan interview with Scottie Pippen, "Olympic Big Shots: Pip, Pip . . . Hooray," *Sports Illustrated for Kids*, July 1, 1996, p. 64.

48. Michael Jordan, "How the Game Has Evolved," The Official Michael Jordan Website-Sportsline USA, cbs.sportsline.com/u/jordan/offcourt/index.html.

49. "Michael Jordan Criticizes Younger Players," The Associated Press, November 17, 1998.

50. Ibid.

51. Melissa Isaccson, "His Airness Shows He's Human," *Chicago Tribune* (Internet Edition), March 20, 1995.

Zen and the Art of Basketball

1. Phil Jackson and Hugh Delehanty, *Sacred Hoops: Spiritual Lessons of a Hardwood Warrior* (New York: Hyperion, 1995), p. 174.

2. Ahmad Rashad interview with Michael Jordan, "1998 Finals: Ahmad Talks with MJ, www.nba.com/mjretirement, 1999.

3. Michael Jordan, *Rare Air* (San Francisco: Collins Publishers San Francisco, 1993), p 17.

4. Melissa Isaacson, "Head Master," *Sporting News*, April 27, 1998.

5. Gary Hill, "NBA-Michael Jordan Outdoes Himself," Reuters, June 15, 1998.

6. Mike Kahn, "Jordan Just Playing, Living for the Moment," CBS Sportsline, cbs. sportsline.com//I/jordan/offcourt/index, html, November 24, 1997.

7. Gary Hill, "NBA-Jordan Has 'Cute' Moment at Eye of Storm," Reuters, June 13, 1998.

8. Michael Jordan, *Rare Air* (San Francisco: Collins Publishers San Francisco, 1993), p. 89.

9. Mark Vancil, "Michael Jordan (interview)," *Playboy*, May 1992, p. 64.

10. Bernie Miklasz, "Jordan Is Mixing Drive and Relaxation in Approach to Finals," *St. Louis Post-Dispatch*, June 7, 1998, p. F1.

11. Ibid.

12. Phil Jackson and Hugh Delehanty, *Sacred Hoops: Spiritual Lessons of a Hardwood Warrior* (New York: Hyperion, 1995), p. 175.

13. Bob Greene, *Rebound: The Odyssey of Michael Jordan* (New York: Viking, 1995), p. 36.

Jordan's Darkest Hours

1. Richard Demak, "Michael Jordan's Long Season," *Sports Illustrated*, March 30, 1992, p. 7.

2. Jimmy Greenfield, "His Greatest Blunders," *Chicago Tribune*, January 14, 1999.

3. Richard Demak, "The Investigation," *Sports Illustrated*, April 13, 1992, p. 11.

4. Richard Demak, "Michael Jordan's Long Season," *Sports Illustrated*, March 30, 1992, p. 7.

5. "Jordan Comes Clean in Court about Debt," Associated Press, *Newsday*, October 23, 1992, p. 171.

6. Ibid.

7. Ibid.

8. Ibid.

9. "Arena (wire and staff reports)," *Newsday*, October 24, 1992.

10. Dave Anderson, "Jordan Can't Slam Dunk Golf Balls," *New York Times*, March 25, 1992.

11. Melissa Isaacson, "Angry Jordan Denies Gambling Charges," *Chicago Tribune*, May 28, 1998.

12. Ibid.

13. Ibid.

14. "Michael Jordan's Dad Found Dead," Associated Press, *San Diego Union-Tribune*, August 13, 1993.

15. "Jordan Calls Gambling Book 'Sensationalized,'" *Chicago Tribune* (from news services), June 5, 1993.

16. Jan Hubbard, "NBA Finals: Jordan's Gambling Non-Issue," *Newsday*, June 11, 1993.

17. Jimmy Greenfield, "His Greatest Blunders," *Chicago Tribune*, January 14, 1999.

18. "NBA Lets Jordan Off the Hook," Associated Press, *Newsday*, October 9, 1993.

19. "Sorry, the First Lady Is Already Taken," *Minneapolis Star Tribune*, October 13, 1995, p. 2C.

20. Dan Barreiro, "Flu-ridden Jordan Leaves Jazz with Sick Feeling," *Minneapolis Star Tribune*, June 12, 1997.

21. Marty Burns, "Jordanalia," *Sports Illustrated*, January 20, 1999, p. 8.

22. Jan Hubbard, "NBA Finals: Jordan's Gambling Non-Issue," *Newsday*, June 11, 1993.

23. Jimmy Greenfield, "His Greatest Blunders," *Chicago Tribune*, January 14, 1999.

24. C.J. Clemmons, "Family Keeps Grief Out of Spotlight," *Newsday*, August 16, 1993.

25. Ibid.

26. Curtis L. Taylor, "Jordan Breaks Silence on Death," *Newsday*, August 20, 1993.

27. Tom Cushman, "Michael Jordan Retires," *San Diego Union-Tribune*, October 7, 1993.

28. C.J. Clemmons, "Family Keeps Grief Out of Spotlight," *Newsday*, August 16, 1993.

29. Curtis L. Taylor, "Jordan Breaks Silence on Death," *Newsday*, August 20, 1993.

30. Melissa Isaacson, *Transition Game: An Inside Look at Life with the Chicago Bulls* (Champaign, IL: Sagamore Publishing, 1994), p. 17.

31. Brant Clifton, "Judge Allows Testimony on Jordan Murder," Reuters, January 25, 1996.

32. William Scally, "Judge in Jordan Trial Says No to Video," Reuters, February 14, 1996.

33. James Bolden, "Michael Jordan Reflects on Past Year," *Los Angeles Sentinel*, July 28, 1994.

34. "Year after Murder, Jordan Still Mourns," Associated Press, *San Diego Union-Tribune*, p. C-8.

35. Mark Jacobson, "Smell Like Mike," *Esquire*, January 1, 1997.

36. Karen M. Thomas, "She Taught Mike What to Be Like," *Dallas Morning News*, August 21, 1996, p. 1C.

37. Bob Greene, *Rebound: The Odyssey of Michael Jordan* (New York: Viking, 1995), p. 36.

38. Melissa Isaacson, *Transition Game: An Inside Look at Life with the Chicago Bulls* (Champaign, IL: Sagamore Publishing, 1994), p. 26.

39. "Chicago: Bulls to Spend $4 Million on Tribute to Jordan's Dad," *Chicago Weekend*, October 30, 1994.

40. Buster Olney, "Jordan Doesn't Rule Out Return," *San Diego Union-Tribune*, October 7, 1993.

41. Franklin Wong, "The World's Greatest Man on Air Returns," *Sun Reporter*, October 26, 1995.

42. E.M. Swift, "Sink, Blast You!" *Sports Illustrated*, August 14, 1989, p. 36.

43. Melissa Isaacson, *Transition Game: An Inside Look at Life with the Chicago Bulls* (Champaign, IL: Sagamore Publishing, 1994), p. 10.

44. "Jordan: NBA at 50 Interview, Part 2," www.nba.com/mjretirement, 1999.

45. Buster Olney, "Jordan Doesn't Rule Out Return," *San Diego Union-Tribune*, October 7, 1993.

46. Ibid.

47. Rick Telander, "Point After: Any of You Sports Fans in Other Cities Had a Tough Couple of Days," *Sports Illustrated*, October 18, 1993, p. 108.

48. Warren Davies, "Basketball Waits Patiently for Jordan's Return," *Weekly Journal*, October 14, 1993.

49. Greg Logan, "Great Moves—Jim Brown Left on Top and Stayed Retired. Can Jordan Do the Same?" *Newsday*, October 10, 1993, p. 32.

50. Dan Bickley, "Air Ego, It's Jordan at the Bat in Chicago," *Newsday*, February 8, 1994, p. 143.

51. Ibid.

52. Ibid.

53. Dan O'Neill, "In General, the White Sox Liked Mike," *St. Louis Post-Dispatch*, March 23, 1994, p. 5D.

54. Ibid.

55. Paul Sullivan, "The 'Other' Career," *Chicago Tribune*, January 14, 1999.

56. "The One and Only," *People Weekly*, January 25, 1999, p. 56.

57. Ray Marsh, "Jordan: Baseball's Air Apparent," *Weekly Journal*, September 29, 1994.

58. Paul Sullivan, "The 'Other' Career," *Chicago Tribune*, January 14, 1999.

59. Ivan Maisel, "College Basketball: Famous N.C. Alumnus Needs No Introduction," *Newsday*, January 11, 1995.

60. Paul Sullivan, "Is White Sox's Loss the Bulls' Gain?" *Chicago Tribune*, March 11, 1995.

61. Ray Marsh, "Jordan: Baseball's Air Apparent," *Weekly Journal*, September 29, 1994.

62. Paul Sullivan, "The 'Other' Career," *Chicago Tribune*, January 14, 1999.

63 Ibid.

64. Melissa Isaacson, "His Airness Shows He's Human," *Chicago Tribune*, March 20, 1995.

65. Rick Weinberg, "A New Ball Game: Michael Jordan Fields Questions about His Struggles on the Diamond and His Potential Return to the NBA," *Sport*, April 1995, p. 26.

66. Franklin Wong, "The World's Greatest Man on Air Returns," *Sun Reporter*, October 26, 1995.

67. David Moore, "Bulls' Jordan Wants to Work His Way Back to the Top," *St. Louis Post-Dispatch*, November 26, 1995.

68. Mark Vancil, "Michael Jordan (interview)," *Playboy*, May 1992, p. 51.

69. Jon Heyman, "World Series/Extra Bases," *Newsday*, October 29, 1995.

The NBA Comeback

1. "Student Briefing Page on the News," *Newsday*, January 19, 1995.

2. Nancy Ryan, "Holding Its Breath, City Waits for Word," *Chicago Tribune*, March 11, 1995, p. 1.

3. Mike Lupica, "Air Back in Bulls' Sails? Michael Couldn't Replace First Love," *Newsday*, March 10, 1995.

4. Sam Smith, *Second Coming: The Strange Odyssey of Michael Jordan: From Courtside to Home Plate and Back Again* (New York: HarperCollins, 1995), p. 90.

5. Ibid., p. 91.

6. Melissa Isaacson, "His Airness Shows He's Human," *Chicago Tribune*, March 20, 1995.

7. Ibid.

8. Ibid.

9. David Moore, "Bulls' Jordan Wants to Work His Way Back to the Top," *St. Louis Post-Dispatch*, November 26, 1995.

10. Mike Kahn, "Jordan Just Playing, Living for the Moment," CBS SportsLine, cbs.sportsline.com/u./jordan/offcourt/index.html, November 24, 1997.

11. Steve Aschburner, "Boorish Behavior Helps Mourning to Get His Way," *Minneapolis Star Tribune*, November 5, 1995.

12. Sam Smith, "Magic, Michael Showdown Fizzles," *Chicago Tribune*, March 2, 1996.

13. Ibid.

14. Melissa Isaacson, "He's Baaaaack," *Chicago Tribune*, March 29, 1995.

15. Ibid.

16. Sam Smith, "Poof! Bulls Vanish with a Whimper," *Chicago Tribune*, May 19, 1995.

17. Spike Lee, *Best Seat in the House: A Basketball Memoir* (New York: Crown Publishers Inc., 1997), p. 238.

18. Shaun Powell, "NBA Taking Up Air Time?" *Newsday*, October 8, 1995.

19. Sam Smith, "Jordan Back—As MVP," *Chicago Tribune*, March 12, 1996.

20. Ibid.

21. Michael Jordan, *For the Love of the Game: My Story* (New York: Crown Publishers, Inc., 1998), p. 131.

22. Allan Wolper, "On the Sports Page," *Editor & Publisher*, December 27, 1997.

Revolutionizing the Sports Economy

1. Spike Lee, *Best Seat in the House: A Basketball Memoir* (New York: Crown Publishers, 1997), pp. 272–274.

2. "Yikes! Mike Takes a Hike," *Business Week*, January 15, 1999, p. 74.

3. "Jordan: NBA at 50 Interview, Part 1," www.nba.com/mjretirement, 1999.

4. Marlene Zeddies and Nick Friedman, "Do Good Guys Wear Black? We Answer the Oddest Questions about Sports Uniforms," *Sports Illustrated for Kids*, October 1, 1997, p. 30.

5. Donald Katz, "Bonus Piece," *Sports Illustrated*, August 16, 1993, p. 54.

6. Michael Jordan, *For the Love of the Game: My Story* (New York: Crown Publishers, Inc., 1998), p. 19.

7. Skip Wollenberg, "Will Public Stay Bullish on Mike?" *Minneapolis Star Tribune*, January 13, 1999.

8. Spike Lee, *Best Seat in the House: A Basketball Memoir* (New York: Crown Publishers, Inc., 1997), p. 135.

9. Skip Myslenski, "Jordan, Dream Team Have Golden Glow," *Chicago Tribune*, August 9, 1996.

10. Donald Katz, "Bonus Piece," *Sports Illustrated*, August 16, 1993, p. 54.

11. Jan Hubbard interview with Michael Jordan, "One on One," *Newsday*, November 27, 1992.

12. Donald Katz, "Bonus Piece," *Sports Illustrated*, August 16, 1993, p. 54.

13. "Air Jordan on the Air," *Chicago Tribune*, July 17, 1998.

14. Henry Louis Gates Jr., "Net Worth: How the Greatest Player in the History of Basketball Became the Greatest Brand in the History of Sports," *New Yorker*, June 1, 1998, p. 48.

15. Curry Kirkpatrick, "In an Orbit All His Own," *Sports Illustrated*, November 9, 1987, p. 82.

16. Harry Berkowitz, "Air's $$$: The Sky's the Limit," *Newsday*, March 10, 1995.

17. Harry Berkowitz, "Serious Error, But a Funny Ad," *Newsday*, March 4, 1995, p. A4.

18. Verena Dobnik, "Nike Takes Hit in Vietnam Labor Report," Associated Press, March 28, 1997, www.saigon.com.

19. Bob Baum, "Jordan's Critics Say It Must Be the Shoes," Associated Press, June 6, 1996, www.saigon.com.

20. Chris Wallace, Diane Sawyer, Sam Donaldson, "Michael Jordan, CEO," *ABC Primetime Live*, November 3, 1997.

21. Garry Trudeau, "Doonesbury" cartoon strip, *Los Angeles Times*, February 22, 1999.

22. Bob Greene, *Hang Time* (New York: Doubleday, 1993), p. 208.

23. "Michael Jordan Launches New Athletic Clothing and Shoe Line," *Jet*, September 29, 1997, p. 51.

24. Elliott Harris, "Nike Still Likes Mike: Business Is a Pleasure," *Chicago Sun-Times*, January 14, 1999.

25. Edward C. Baig, "Selling: ProServ Wins a Big One in Sports Marketing," *Fortune*, September 30, 1985.

26. Steve Marantz, "The Power of Air," *Sporting News*, December 22, 1997, p. 12.

27. Nancy Armour, "Who Will Rise to the Throne of His Airness?" *North County Times*, January 14, 1999, p. C5.

28. Michael Jordan, *Rare Air* (San Francisco: Collins Publishers San Francisco, 1993), p. 49.

29. Steve Marantz, "The Power of Air," *Sporting News*, December 22, 1997, p. 12.

30. Deloris Jordan, *Family First: Winning the Parenting Game* (San Francisco: Harper San Francisco, 1996), p. 147.

31. Wayne Friedman, "Jordan the Star Athlete Retires, Jordan the Brand Comes to Life," *Advertising Age*, January 18, 1999, p. 3.

32. "Yikes! Mike Takes a Hike," *Business Week*, January 25, 1999, p. 74.

33. "Scorecard," *Sports Illustrated*, October 18, 1993, p. 23.

34. Roy S. Johnson, "The Jordan Effect: The World's Greatest Basketball Player Is Also One of Its Great Brands. What Is His Impact on the Economy?" *Fortune*, June 22, 1998.

35. Ibid.

36. Ibid.

37. Ibid.

38. Gary Hill, "NBA-Michael Jordan Outdoes Himself Again," Reuters, June 15, 1998.

39. Ed Sherman, "Where's the MJ Touch?" *Chicago Tribune*, July 14, 1998.

40. Bob Logan, "Rookie Signs for $6 Million," *Chicago Tribune*, September 13, 1984.

41. Rick Telander, "Ready . . . Set . . . Levitate! Midair Is the Lofty Realm of Chicago's Michael Jordan, and He has Lifted the Bulls Off to a Stratospheric Start," *Sports Illustrated*, November 17, 1986, p. 16.

42. Peter Spiegel, "Jordan & Co.," *Forbes*, December 15, 1997, p. 180.

43. Chris Wallace, Diane Sawyer, Sam Donaldson, "Michael Jordan, CEO," *ABC Primetime Live*, November 3, 1997.

44. Mark Vancil, Michael Jordan (interview), *Playboy*, May 1992, p. 51.

45. Jack McCallum, "Horns of a Dilemma; Michael Jordan Continues to Carry the Bulls, But How Much Abuse Can His Body Take?" *Sports Illustrated*, March 13, 1989, p. 34.

46. Henry Louis Gates Jr., "Net Worth: How the Greatest Player in the History of Basketball Became the Greatest Brand in the History of Sports," *New Yorker*, June 1, 1998, p. 48.

47. Joe Gergen, "Sunday Special: Jordan Air of Uncertainty," *Newsday*, May 25, 1997.

48. Ibid.

49. "Advisory: Jordan Faces Estate Planning Needs," Business Wire, January 14, 1999.

50. Michael Jordan, *For the Love of the Game: My Story* (New York: Crown Publishers, Inc., 1998), p. 118.

51. Simeon Gant, "Jordan and Group Dislike NBA Agreement," *Sacramento Observer*, August 23, 1995.

52. Hal Bock, "Michael Jordan Convinced . . . Players Association Should Go," *New York Beacon*, August 9, 1995.

53. Shaun Powell, "Unity in Union?" *Newsday*, September 13, 1995, p. 68.

54. Rob Parker, "Style Points by Jordan, Ewing," *Newsday*, September 13, 1995.

55. "Jordan Claims Loss of Season Would Erode Skills," *Minneapolis Star Tribune*, September 8, 1995, p. 8C.

56. "We Have to Stand for What We Believe In," Associated Press, www.cnnsi.com, October 23, 1998.

57. Elizabeth Vargas interview with Scottie Pippen, ABC's *Good Morning America*, January 13, 1999.

58. Michael Jordan Retirement Press Conference, January 13, 1999.

59. Ibid.

60. Ray Marsh, "Charity Begins at Home for Michael Jordan," *Weekly Journal*, December 8, 1994.

61. "Michael's Fundamentals Backed by Jordan," Interactive Sports Wire, www.comtexnews.com, February 3, 1999.

62. Andrew Kilpatrick, *Of Permanent Value: The Story of Warren Buffett* (Birmingham, AL: AKPE, 1998), pp. 144–145.

As Famous as God?

1. "Powell, Woods, Jordan, Most Popular Americans," *Jet*, May 19, 1997, p. 5.

2. "Jordan: NBA at 50 Interview, Part 2," www.nba.com/mjretirement, 1999.

3. Steve Marantz, "The Power of Air," *Sporting News*, December 22, 1997, p. 12.

4. Sal Maiorana, "Jordan's 63-Point Playoff Outburst against the Celtics," Sportsline USA, 1998.

5. Mark Heisler, "Memories: This Is Greatness No One Could Pin Down," *Los Angeles Times*, January 13, 1999, p. D1.

6. Phil Hersh, "Should His Airness Be a Cultural Icon?" *Chicago Tribune*, March 24, 1995.

7. Bob Sakamoto, "He Was a Carefree Kid Who Loved to Play," *Chicago Tribune*, March 21, 1996.

8. Mark Heisler, "Memories: This Is Greatness No One Could Pin Down," January 13, 1999, *Los Angeles Times*, p. D1.

9. Kevin Cook, Michael Jordan (interview), *Playboy*, March 1997, p. 122.

10. Michael O'Leary, "War Music" (book review), *Chicago Review*, September 22, 1997, pp. 152–155.

11. Bob Greene, *Hang Time* (New York: Doubleday, 1992), p. 154.

12. Mike Lupica, "The Greatest Show on Ice: After a Legendary Career on the Road, Wayne Gretzky Finally Takes His Act to New York," *Esquire*, January 1, 1997, pp. 40–42.

13. Allan Wolper, "On the Sports Page," *Editor & Publisher*, December 27, 1997.

14. Sam Smith, *Second Coming: The Strange Odyssey of Michael Jordan: From Courtside to Home Plate and Back Again* (New York: HarperCollins Publishers, 1995), p. xiii.

15. Phil Hersh, "Should His Airness Be a Cultural Icon?" *Chicago Tribune*, March 24, 1995.

16. Michael Jordan, *Rare Air* (San Francisco: Collins Publishers San Francisco, 1993), p. 43.

17. Mike Lupica, "Damn Bulls," *Esquire*, May 1, 1997, p. 44.

18. Bob Sakamoto, "He was a Carefree Kid Who Loved to Play," *Chicago Tribune*, March 21, 1996.

19. Mark Vancil, Michael Jordan (interview), *Playboy*, May 1992, p. 51.

20. Rick Reilly, "Pro Basketball: Last Call? The Greatest Sports Dynasty of the '90s May (or May Not) Be about to Hang It Up, but Behind the Scenes the Chicago Bulls' Season Has Certainly Felt Like a Farewell Tour," *Sports Illustrated*, May 11, 1998, p. 32.

21. "The Door," ABC News *Nightline*, November 13, 1998, www.ABC.com.

22. "Jordan Remembers Times before Jordan-Mania," Associated Press, cbs.sportsline.com/I/jordan/offcourt/index.html, 1998.

23. Jack McCallum, "Air Jordan, Air Bulls," *Sports Illustrated*, May 16, 1988, p. 32.

24. Bob Greene, *Rebound: The Odyssey of Michael Jordan* (New York: Viking, 1995), pp. 38–39.

25. Rick Telander, "I'd Rather Look Back Than Ahead," *Chicago Sun-Times*, January 13, 1999.

26. Mark Vancil, Michael Jordan (interview), *Playboy*, May 1992, p. 51.

27. Mark Alesia, "Before Jordan Had an 'Air' About Him . . . ," cbs.sportsline.com/I/jordan/offcourt/index.html, May 11, 1998.

28. "Fake Memorabilia," *Upper Deck*, December 15, 1997.

29. Auctions: Antiques & Collectibles: Trading Cards: Basketball: Singles: Michael Jordan, auctions.yahoo.com/21026-category-leaf.html.

30. "This Week's Sign That the Apocalypse Is Upon Us," *Sports Illustrated*, June 16, 1997.

31. "Retired Jordan Jersey Lifted from Rafters at UNC," Reuters, February 4, 1998.

32. Rick Telander, "Senseless," *Sports Illustrated*, May 14, 1990, p. 36.

33. Associated Press, "Tallish Gentleman in North Carolina Has Certain Air about Him," *San Diego Union-Tribune*, January 21, 1999.

34. William Power, "No Bull: Michael Jordan Is Still Suiting Up for Basketball Games," *Wall Street Journal*, January 21, 1999, p. B1.

35. Jean Bethke Elshtain, "The Hard Questions," *The New Republic*, March 31, 1997.

36. Mark Vancil, Michael Jordan (interview), *Playboy*, May 1992, p. 51.

The Man behind the Idol

1. Michael Kiefer, "Air Attack; Flying High in Points and Profits, Michael Jordan Is the Jam Master of the NBA," *Playboy*, April 1988, p. 80.

2. Rick Telander, "I'd Rather Look Back Than Ahead," *Chicago Sun-Times*, January 13, 1999.

3. Sam Smith, *Second Coming: The Strange Odyssey of Michael Jordan—From Courtside to Home Plate and Back Again* (New York: HarperCollins Publishers, 1995), p. 108.

4. Roland Lazenby, "Another Side of Michael," *Sport*, June 1998, p. 46.

5. Jack McCallum, "That's Cold, Man," *Sports Illustrated*, February 18, 1991, p. 58.

6. Franklin Wong, "The World's Greatest Man on Air Returns," *Sun Reporter*, October 26, 1995.

7. J.A. Adande, "Memories: Obscure Moment Symbolizes the Greatest," *Los Angeles Times*, January 13, 1999, p. D1.

8. Marty Burns, "Jordanalia," *Sports Illustrated*, January 20, 1999.

9. Kent McDill, "Players Have to Be 'Immune' to Verbal Lashes," CBS Sportsline, cbs.sportsline.com/I/jordan/offcourt/index.html, 1998.

10. Sam Smith, *Second Coming: The Strange Odyssey of Michael Jordan—From Courtside to Home Plate and Back Again* (New York: HarperCollins Publishers, 1995), p. xvi.

11. Roland Lazenby, "Another Side of Michael," *Sport*, June 1998, p. 46.

12. Skip Bayless, "That Nasty Side to Jordan Helped Make Him Great," *Chicago Tribune*, January 17, 1999.

13. Allison Samuels, interview with Michael Jordan, "Mike on Mike," *Newsweek*, September 22, 1997.

14. Barry Jacobs, "High-flying Michael Jordan Has North Carolina Cruising Toward Another NCAA Title," *People Weekly*, March 19, 1984, p. 42.

15. Jack McCallum, "Horns of a Dilemma; Michael Jordan Continues to Carry the Bulls, But How Much Abuse Can His Body Take?" *Sports Illustrated*, February 18, 1991, p. 34.

16. Michael Kiefer, "Air Attack; Flying High in Points and Profits, Michael Jordan Is the Jam Master of the NBA," *Playboy*, April 1988, p. 80.

17. Lynn Norment, "Michael and Juanita Jordan Talk about Love, Marriage and Life after Basketball," *Ebony*, November 1991, p. 68.

18. Ibid.

19. Michael Kiefer, "Air Attack; Flying High in Points and Profits, Michael Jordan Is the Jam Master of the NBA," *Playboy*, April 1988, p. 80.

20. Mitchel Krugel, *Jordan: The Man, His Words, His Life* (New York: St. Martin's Press, 1994), p. 233.

21. Ibid.

22. Lynn Norment, "Michael and Juanita Jordan Talk about Love, Marriage and Life after Basketball," *Ebony*, November 1991, p. 68.

23. Deloris Jordan, *Family First: Winning the Parenting Game* (New York: Harper San Francisco, 1996), p. 33.

24. Steve Aschburner, "Crank Call to Jordan Disrupts Bulls' Game," cbs.sportsline.com/I/jordan/offcourt/index.html, December 30, 1997.

25. Michael Jordan retirement press conference, *CNN*, January 13, 1999.

26. Bob Sakamoto, "He Was a Carefree Kid Who Loved to Play," *Chicago Tribune*, March 21, 1996.

27. Michael Kiefer, "Air Attack; Flying High in Points and Profits, Michael Jordan Is the Jam Master of the NBA," *Playboy*, April 1988, p. 80.

28. Curry Kirkpatrick, "In an Orbit All His Own," *Sports Illustrated*, November 9, 1987, p. 82.

29. Daniel Ames, "M.J." *Sports Illustrated for Kids*, August 1997, p. 73.

30. Steve Aschburner, "Bulls Are Back, and So Are Same Stories," *Star Tribune*, June 4, 1997.

31. CBS Sportsline, America Online, March 22, 1999

32. "Air Time: Kids Ask Michael Jordan about Hoops and Life," *Sports Illustrated for Kids*, March 1996, p. 32.

33. Marty Burns, "Jordanalia," *Sports Illustrated*, January 20, 1999, p. 8.

34. Rick Telander, "Ready . . . Set . . . Levitate! Midair Is the Lofty Realm of Chicago's Michael Jordan, and He Has Lifted the Bulls Off to a Stratospheric Start," *Sports Illustrated*, November 17, 1986, p. 16.

35. Ibid.

36. Mark Vancil, Michael Jordan (interview), *Playboy*, May 1992, p. 51.

37. Bob Sakamoto, "Family Is at the Core of Jordan's Dream," *Chicago Tribune*, April 15, 1990.

38. Ibid.

39. Phil Hersh, "Should His Airness Be a Cultural Icon?" *Chicago Tribune*, March 24, 1995.

40. Charles Barkley with Rick Reilly, *Sir Charles: The Wit and Wisdom of Charles Barkley* (New York: Time Warner Books, 1994), p. 40.

41. George Nelson, "Rare Jordan: Soaring," *Essence*, November 1, 1996, pp. 106–108.

42. Fred Mitchell, "His Inner Circle," *Chicago Tribune*, January 17, 1999.

43. J.A. Adande, "No News Is Good News," *Los Angeles Times*, January 14, 1999, p. D1.

44. Fred Mitchell, "His Inner Circle," *Chicago Tribune*, January 17, 1999.

45. Mark Vancil, Michael Jordan (interview), *Playboy*, May 1992, p. 51.

46. Jack McCallum, "Horns of a Dilemma; Michael Jordan Continues to Carry the Bulls, But How Much Abuse Can His Body Take?" *Sports Illustrated*, March 13, 1989, p. 34.

47. E.M. Swift, "Sink, Blast You!" *Sports Illustrated*, August 14, 1989, p. 36.

48. Ibid.

49. Ed Sherman, "View from the Green," *Chicago Tribune*, January 14, 1999.

50. Thomas Bonk, "Jolly Green Giants: Jordan Swings Easily into Retirement on a Laugh-Filled Day in Desert," *Los Angeles Times*, January 21, 1999.

Michael Jordan in Hollywood

1. Kevin Cook, Michael Jordan (interview), *Playboy*, March 1997, p. 122.

2. Kate Meyers, "Court Jester," *Entertainment Weekly*, November 22, 1996.

3. Ibid.

4. Ibid.

5. "Who's Number One? Your Votes Are In! What You Told Us in Our Latest Readers' Poll," *Sports Illustrated for Kids*, March 1, 1998.

6. Kate Meyers, "Court Jester," *Entertainment Weekly*, November 22, 1996.

7. Eric Fidler, "Jury Finds for Michael Jordan," Associated Press, October 16, 1998.

The Jordan End Game

1. Jack McCallum, "Horns of a Dilemma; Michael Jordan Continues to Carry the Bulls, but How Much Abuse Can His Body Take?" *Sports Illustrated*, March 13, 1989, p. 34.

2. Michael Jordan retirement press conference, CNN, January 13, 1999.

3. Sam Smith, "Three Little Words," *Chicago Tribune*, January 28, 1999.

4. Jan Hubbard interview with Michael Jordan, "One on One," *Newsday*, November 11, 1992.

5. Jeff Coplon, "Legends. Champions?" *New York Times Magazine*, April 21, 1996, p. 32.

6. Ahmad Rashad with Michael Jordan, "1998 Finals: Ahmad Talks with MJ," www.nba.com/mjretirement, 1999.

7 Gary Hill, "NBA-Jordan Loves Proving the Doubters Wrong," Reuters, June 8, 1998.

8. Ibid.

9. Lacy J. Banks, "'I'm Better Than Ever.' A Tough Workout Regimen Keeps Michael Jordan Fit Enough to Defy Age and Opponents Alike," *Sport*, June 1997, p. 21.

10. Kent McDill, "Will Jordan Stay or Will He Go?" The Official Michael Jordan Web site, Sportsline USA, cbs.sportsline.com/I/jordan/offcourt/index.html, March 22, 1998.

11. Dave Krieger, "Bulls Seek to Avoid Crossing Signals," *Denver Rocky Mountain News*, October 12, 1997.

12. Greg Beacham, "Jordan Reiterates His Threat to Retire," *The Columbian*, February 5, 1998.

13. Kent McDill, "Will Jordan Stay or Will He Go?" The Official Michael Jordan Web site, Sportsline USA, cbs.sportsline.com/I/jordan/offcourt/index.html, March 22, 1998.

14. Ibid.

15. "Leaning Toward Retirement," Associated Press, www.cnnsi.com, July 16, 1998.

16. Ibid.

17. Lacy J. Banks, "It's Official: MJ's Gone," *Chicago Sun-Times*, January 13, 1999.

18. John Dempsey, "NBC Still Hopes to Take Jordan into Overtime," *Variety*, July 27, 1998, p. 3.

19. Kent McDill, "Jordan Loves the Game, Resents Playing Games," CBS Sportsline, cbs.sportsline.com/I/jordan/offcourt/index.html, December 14, 1997.

20. Ken Vance, "Jordan Has a Field Day—Again," *The Columbian*, January 30, 1998.

21. Rick Reilly, "Pro Basketball: Last Call? The Greatest Sports Dynasty of the '90s May (or May Not) Be About to Hang It Up, But Behind the Scenes the Chicago Bulls' Season Has Certainly Felt Like a Farewell Tour," *Sports Illustrated*, May 11, 1998, p. 32.

22. Ibid.

23. "Key Dates," *Los Angeles Times*, January 11, 1999, p. D11.

24. Sam Smith, "Tense Bulls Drama: Waiting for Michael," *Chicago Tribune*, January 8, 1999.

25. Sam Smith, "What's Wrong with the Bulls?" *The Sporting News*, November 24, 1997.

26. David Stern, *Larry King Live*, CNN, January 5, 1999.

27. John Maffei, "Jordan's Coverage Bigger Than Kennedy Assassination," *North County Times*, January 15, 1999, p. C–5.

28. Jay Mariotti, "Perfect Ending: MJ Goes Out on Top," *Chicago Sun-Times*, January 13, 1999.

29. Tom Cushman, "Spotlight's Glare Too Much to Bear for Man Called Air," *San Diego Union-Tribune*, October 7, 1993.

30. Michael Jordan retirement press conference, CNN, January 13, 1999.

31. Jim O'Donnell, "The Stuff of an NBA Legend," *Chicago Sun-Times*, January 13, 1999.

32. Charles Barkley with Rick Reilly, *Sir Charles: The Wit and Wisdom of Charles Barkley*, (New York: Warner Books, 1994), p. 9.

33. Michael Jordan retirement press conference, CNN, January 13, 1999.

34. Ibid.

35. Ibid.

36. Ibid.

37. Ibid.

38. "Leaning Toward Retirement," Associated Press, www.cnnsi.com, July 26, 1998.

39. Mike Kahn, "Jordan Just Playing, Living for the Moment," CBS Sportsline, cbs.sportsline.com/I/jordan/offcourt/index.html, November 24, 1997.

40. Rick Weinberg, "A New Ball Game: Michael Jordan Fields Questions about His Struggles on the Diamond and His Potential Return to the NBA," *Sport*, April 1995, p. 26.

41. "Michael Jordan Says His Ultimate Dream Is to Spend More Time 'Watching My Kids Grow Up,'" *Jet*, March 9, 1998, p. 34.

42. Michael Jordan, America Online Sportsline, March 22, 1999.

43. Elizabeth Vargas interview with Bob Greene, ABC *Good Morning America*, January 13, 1999.